WINNIPEG
AUG 11 2010
PUBLIC LIBRARY
WITHDRAWN

"It's hard to resist a gardening book that's both chock-full of information and fun to read. It doesn't matter if you are a novice gardener or more experienced, Annie shows the way to growing and enjoying a natural, sustainable, organic garden."

　　　　—Nell Newman, cofounder and president of Newman's Own Organics

"Annie Spiegelman (aka the Dirt Diva) understands what gardening is *really* about: having fun . . . even when you aren't having fun! This book is laugh-out-loud useful and smart. Frankly, it's the best book on organic gardening that I've seen in 11 years (since mine came out). The Dirt Diva Royal Horticultural Society is the only gardening club I really want to be a member of."

　　　　—Maria Rodale, CEO of Rodale Inc., MariasFarmCountryKitchen.com

"*Talking Dirt* is wonderful—even for those who don't have a garden . . . yet."　　　　—Christiane Northrup, MD, author of the *New York Times* bestsellers *Women's Bodies, Women's Wisdom* and *The Wisdom of Menopause*

"Fun, factual, and filled with ideas. What sets *Talking Dirt* apart from all other organic gardening how-to guides is Anne Spiegelman. Her writing has an easy style, is easy to understand, and makes organic gardening easy to put into practice. The information is presented with personality and wit, making this book a must-have resource for the aspiring organic gardener."

　　　　—Michael C. Metallo, president of the National Gardening Association

"Beautifully combining passion, humor, and a deep-rooted care for the planet, Spiegelman is the organic femme fatale. She understands the importance of our own backyards to build a better future, one shovelful of compost at a time. What a funtastic book."

　　　　—Helge Hellberg, executive director of Marin Organic, host of *An O...*

continued . . .

D1018653

"What *Skinny Bitch* did for vegetarianism *Talking Dirt* may do for organic gardening. Annie Spiegelman's book is the perfect primer for a generation raised on supermarket food and flowers but who are searching for something fresher and more satisfying. As comfortable among the cabbages as she is in a fashion boutique, Spiegelman succeeds in making the intricacies of gardening without toxic chemicals exciting and rewarding. With a light, swift tone and ample instruction, this is the organic gardening book for busy people."

—Brian Clark Howard, environmental journalist and
web editor for *The Daily Green*

"Spiegelman's tone is reminiscent of the 'Samurai Shopper' column in the *New York Times* . . . entertaining and effective."

—Brian Halweil, author of *Eat Here* and senior researcher
for World Watch Institute

"Spiegelman tells the lighthearted story of her own transformation from weekend gardener to a 'Dirt Diva.' *Talking Dirt* is full of tips all gardeners should take to heart to make their plot organic and nurture their plants the way nature intended."

—Tom Szaky, CEO and founder of TerraCycle Inc.

TALKING DIRT

The Dirt Diva's
Down-to-Earth Guide to
Organic Gardening

ANNIE SPIEGELMAN
Illustrations by Maggie Agro

A PERIGEE BOOK

A PERIGEE BOOK
Published by the Penguin Group
Penguin Group (USA) Inc.
375 Hudson Street, New York, New York 10014, USA
Penguin Group (Canada), 90 Eglinton Avenue East, Suite 700, Toronto, Ontario M4P 2Y3, Canada
(a division of Pearson Penguin Canada Inc.)
Penguin Books Ltd., 80 Strand, London WC2R 0RL, England
Penguin Group Ireland, 25 St. Stephen's Green, Dublin 2, Ireland (a division of Penguin Books Ltd.)
Penguin Group (Australia), 250 Camberwell Road, Camberwell, Victoria 3124, Australia
(a division of Pearson Australia Group Pty. Ltd.)
Penguin Books India Pvt. Ltd., 11 Community Centre, Panchsheel Park, New Delhi—110 017, India
Penguin Group (NZ), 67 Apollo Drive, Rosedale, North Shore 0632, New Zealand
(a division of Pearson New Zealand Ltd.)
Penguin Books (South Africa) (Pty.) Ltd., 24 Sturdee Avenue, Rosebank, Johannesburg 2196,
South Africa

Penguin Books Ltd., Registered Offices: 80 Strand, London WC2R 0RL, England

While the author has made every effort to provide accurate telephone numbers and Internet addresses at the time of publication, neither the publisher nor the author assumes any responsibility for errors, or for changes that occur after publication. Further, the publisher does not have any control over and does not assume any responsibility for author or third-party websites or their content.

Copyright © 2010 by Annie Spiegelman
Illustrations by Maggie Agro
Cover design by Christian Fuenfhausen
Text design by Tiffany Estreicher

All rights reserved.
No part of this book may be reproduced, scanned, or distributed in any printed or electronic form without permission. Please do not participate in or encourage piracy of copyrighted materials in violation of the author's rights. Purchase only authorized editions.
PERIGEE is a registered trademark of Penguin Group (USA) Inc.
The "P" design is a trademark belonging to Penguin Group (USA) Inc.

First edition: March 2010

Library of Congress Cataloging-in-Publication Data

Spiegelman, Annie.
   Talking dirt : the dirt diva's down-to-earth guide to organic gardening / Annie Spiegelman ;
illustrations by Maggie Agro.— 1st ed.
   p.   cm.
   "A Perigee book."
   Includes index.
   ISBN 978-0-399-53565-9
   1. Organic gardening—Handbooks, manuals, etc.   I. Agro, Maggie.   II. Title.
III. Title: Dirt diva's down-to-earth guide to organic gardening.
   SB453.5.S67 2010
   635'.0484—dc22   2009040346

PRINTED IN THE UNITED STATES OF AMERICA

10 9 8 7 6 5 4 3 2 1

Most Perigee books are available at special quantity discounts for bulk purchases for sales promotions, premiums, fund-raising, or educational use. Special books, or book excerpts, can also be created to fit specific needs. For details, write: Special Markets, Penguin Group (USA) Inc., 375 Hudson Street, New York, New York 10014.

To my dad, Simon Spiegelman,
for teaching me to work hard and aim high, and for taking me
out for coffee when I wasn't in the mood to do either.

ACKNOWLEDGMENTS

A huge bouquet of thanks to my editor, Maria Gagliano, coach, slave driver, and word-pruner extraordinaire. I am grateful to my steadfast literary agents, Sophie McManus and Fredrica Friedman, for having faith that a book about worm worship and soil strategy could stand a chance.

Extra special credit goes to my eco-centric pals: Helge Hellberg, Veronica Valero, Marie Chan, Kimberly Pinkson, Gerald Prolman, Debi Tidd, Gina Purin, Miguel Villarreal, Blair Randall, Jeanne Santangelo, Stephen Andrews, and Lisa Ludwigsen, for inspiring me to step away from the craft service table on the film set and join them in their passionate efforts to create a healthier and sustainable future for us all.

I am indebted to the botanical wizards, farm advisers, soil scientists, and entomologists at the University of California, Davis and Berkeley, and at Cornell University, who returned my calls and explained scientific theories to me in shallow terms that a person coming from the movie industry could digest. I promise I won't call you nerds anymore, and I hope I do your environmental and horticultural explanations justice. (Geeks!)

Kudos to Linda Xiques, past managing editor at the *Pacific Sun*, for giving the Dirt Diva garden column its start, and to Jason Walsh, present editor, for allowing me to continue ranting on behalf of Mother Nature, and for sending me out to write stories on rare, threatened, and endangered plants that haven't been seen or heard of by historical botanists for one hundred years. There will be payback, Jason. (A shout-out to the irrepressible *Pacific Sun* art department!)

I'm a huge fan of the radio station WUMB in Boston. They kept me sane in my backyard office under the redwood tree while writing. Except for the day there was a guy yodeling. Seriously.

Big squeezes to Betty, Elissa, Gwyneth, Barbitchin', Pucci, and Cecily, for all those pep talks and for making me dance and allowing me to bring you buckets of homemade compost tied with a bow. Hugs to my friends and family who've been with me on the rocky path to book deals and beyond: the A List; the Circle; the Santa Cruz Posse; Aunt Ceil and the yummy Feldmans, Rebecca, Madison, Morgan; Virginia Alyea; the superstar sisters-in-law; and my many unruly cohorts in the Bay Area film community, especially Gunderman, Otewalt, Herzig, Condiotti, Mickey Freeman, Lisa Ewald, Brahna Stone, Mindy Hall, and Genevieve "Sister Sledge" Haag. (And Paul Chaput, sort of.) *Where are my people?!*

Thanks to my big sister, Augusta, for leading me into the garden; to my twin sister, Carol, for actually reading my gardening articles; and to my sister, Sharon, for asking, "Why?"

Thank you to Bill, for cheering me on every morning in my writing shed, and for letting me exist in my make-believe, flowery world, as if that were *normal.*

Jack, you'll always be my sunshine (even with your iPod on).

CONTENTS

I had rather be on my farm than be emperor of the world.

—GEORGE WASHINGTON

INTRODUCTION

I can't quite explain how a girl raised and hardened on the streets of New York City became a Master Gardener, passionate environmentalist, and utterly obsessed with old English roses. But it happened, to me.

When I first arrived in northern California, I shared the same enthusiasm for the natural grace and dreamy charms of a perennial cottage garden like so many other wistful gardeners. The problem was the lot I acquired was overgrown with waist-high weeds, shards of old timber and glass, chunks of busted up patio, three sadly worn-out fruit trees, and a large rusty object I never was able to identify. Among the strewn rubble were patches of some old, forgotten, and overcrowded perennial plants. I felt, somehow, I was needed. I was at that moment inspired (some might say possessed) to revive this old abandoned garden.

Of course, having a harebrained idea isn't the same thing as actually making it happen. I had no conceptual clue of what to do or where to start. Back then, I was traveling to Hollywood to work on nonsensical TV movies and on the weekends would flee back home to my garden sanctuary, to cleanse my soul and repent. My two cats would lazily perch on the back deck yawning, as I dug, watered, turned and tossed, cursed and mumbled, and prayed for something, anything to bloom.

After lots of trial and error and a plethora of dead plants petulantly tossed across the yard into the compost pile, I decided it was time to learn how to garden. I walked to the local library and serendipitously stumbled upon an article about the Master Gardening program. Of the character traits sought in a candidate applying to become a Master Gardener, it advised, "must like people" and "get excited by free aged horse manure." I wasn't quite sure if I liked people. However, I was working on it. And then, as if being touched by some saintly horticultural spirit, I instantly got "the manure thrill," though at the time I had absolutely no idea what I was feeling or what I would do with all the animal droppings. The idea of free horse manure, which I'd heard was a zesty crop fertilizer, gave me the same endorphin rush as a Macy's semiannual shoe sale. I knew, at that precise moment, I was destined to metamorphose from a clumsy, challenged, unqualified nymph into a full-fledged, card-carrying Dirt Diva.

Joining the Master Gardener program offered me the opportunity to be tutored by many gifted and distinguished horticultural professors, botanists, farm advisers, soil scientists, and industry experts. They showed me how to create and plant a healthy, flourishing landscape while still remaining ecologically responsible, as I intrepidly forged ahead in my never-ending pursuit of the perfect garden. Their commonsense philosophy was to avoid conventional pesticides, fungicides, and herbicides as a first line of defense against pests or disease. Many of these chemicals are toxic to birds, bees, and other beneficial insects that play an essential role in the garden's ecosystem as pollinators, decomposers, and predators of other pests. The instructors were careful to honorably respect the many and varied gardening viewpoints while offering sound advice that has been scientifically researched and proven to render the least amount of harm to the environment.

That was 10 years ago. Now, despite having planted a variety of somewhat demanding English roses and some nitpicky perennials, I have no need for synthetic fertilizers and other petrochemicals. This time, I went *organic* and beat "the Man." Organic gardening focuses on feeding the *soil* instead of feeding the *plant*. This in turn promotes stronger plants that are less susceptible to insects and disease. If your soil is enriched with decomposed organic matter, your plants will be naturally fed by nutrients released by soil microbes working underground. These underground microorganisms are your people. They're working for you 24/7. They feed your flowers, provide critical minerals for your vegetable crops, and aerate your soil so water can reach the roots.

Trust me, you need these people!

Our ancestors saved seeds; recycled waste; created homemade potions to outwit pests, weeds, and disease; and carefully planned where and when to plant their flower and food crops. Back then this wasn't labeled organic gardening. It was simply a commonsensical, ecological, and responsible approach to sustainably cultivating the land. Not the quick fix–pay later tactic we've become all too naively indoctrinated and enamored by since the rise of the petrochemical industry following World War II.

Being an organic gardener is not about going back in time. This isn't your mother's garden or your grandmother's either. It's simply smart, safe, and sustainable gardening. It also happens to be the fastest-growing segment of the gardening industry and a trend that is expected to increase in the future. Where the money goes, industry follows. Consumers vote with their checkbook. They want gardens that build healthy soil, reduce waste, conserve water, create wildlife habitat, protect local watersheds, and contribute to a healthy community. As award-winning poet, novelist, and farmer Wendell Berry writes, "When going back makes sense, you are going forward."

My garden now has both diversity and balance and has evolved into a naturally sustaining and flourishing ecosystem. That's how forests and meadows grow. There are no elves tiptoeing over the troll bridge with a plastic jug of bright pink fertilizer pellets, a watering can, and a beer.

If a skeptical ex-Manhattanite, formerly entrenched in the maniacal movie industry, can achieve this, trust me . . . you can too. It's not rocket science.

As your cynically optimistic horticultural host, I'll explain why and how to befriend the zillions of fungi, bacteria, and other creepy-crawlers in your soil. You'll learn how to properly build a steaming compost pile, the essentials in designing a small garden, why the earthworm rules, how to attract butterflies and honeybees, how to use cover crops (and I don't mean pot) to invigorate your soil, and different ways to combat weeds and pests.

Feel free to jump around the book if you're merely interested in planting a fruit tree or growing roses. I do ask that before you shuffle off to those pages you first read the chapters on soil and compost in Part One, and take notes! What you obtain from those two chapters will make or break your garden. If you don't continually build, bless, and bolster your soil (the foundation of your garden) with organic matter (compost), you'll simply be wasting your time and money.

Also, at the end of each chapter, I've included a plant recommendation by the not-quite-ready-for-prime-time Dirt Diva Royal Horticultural Society, along with a truly delightful plant drawing by artist Maggie Agro. Each plant recommendation comes with a "Whaaa-whaa rating." My Universal Botanical Whaaa-whaa Rating System rates plants on their practical botanical merit and their level of whining. Do they invite beneficial insects? Are they low-water or low-maintenance plants? Are they dazzling yet pest and disease resistant? Do they make the gardener look like a botanical wizard? Plants that thrive, bloom profusely, and ask little of their caretaker are rated a 1. Conversely, those perpetually hungry, thirsty, and needy plants that invite you to Loser-Land, are relegated a 10. When shopping for plants, remember to keep your score sheet low if you don't want to be trapped in just another codependent relationship.

I truly hope this book inspires experienced garden geeks to continue experimenting with what grows best in their own yards or city rooftop gardens. For novice gardeners, yearning to create your own Garden of Eden, I hope to make the road to a happy, healthy yard a bit less daunting and a lot more pleasurable so you too will one day love gardening as much as us shameless hortiholics.

Gardeners the world over dream of having their own Garden of Paradise. One festooned with colorful climbing vines and sweet peas; breathtakingly beautiful and fragrant roses; fruit trees limb-heavy with fruit; scores of butterflies, bees, and hummingbirds; and a prolific harvest of vegetable crops and scented culinary herbs. It is possible to accomplish all this, but unfortunately, *sigh*, it takes an abundance of hope, hard work, unconditional love, and patience. I have plenty of the first three, but can you find the letter *P* in *DIVA*? I know. I was forced to learn the virtue patience, and I'm still not happy about it. But with some basic gardening skills and knowledge, you'll have a much better chance of successfully creating your own little utopia in an enjoyable and time-conserving way. You'll be working alongside Mother Nature, not against her. The two of you will make your garden a sustainable, naturally fertile, environmentally friendly, and, of course, beautiful ecosystem.

Last, if you remember just one thing from this book, make it this: When in doubt, the answer is always compost and mulch. Repeat after me: COMPOST AND MULCH.

May the force always be with you, my sweet kumquats.

PART ONE

Starting a Spectacular and Sustainable Garden

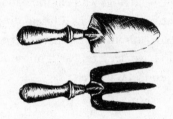

Get ready to learn the basics to growing an environmentally friendly garden. The first few chapters will guide you through planning your garden design, how to use those fancy botanical plant names at the nursery, and which tools you'll need for your long-term love affair with gardening. Not in love with gardening yet? I'll get you there. Come on in. The water's fine!

Probably the most important chapter of the book is Chapter 4, "Talking Dirty: It All Begins with Your Soil." Soil is the most biologically productive ecosystem on the planet. It's what sustains life on our planet, yet we neglect and abuse it. We'd be toast without it. We can't survive with air and water (and the Internet) alone. Entire civilizations have been lost for taking their soil for granted. So, get up. We've got work to do!

In Chapter 5, "Going Compostal," you'll learn how to compost food scraps from your home so they're not adding to our overflowing landfills, which are emitting methane like it's going out of style. It *is* out of style. You'll learn how amending your soil with compost (not chemicals) will keep your soil healthy and productive for years to come, and will make the angels sing. Hallelujah.

In Chapter 6, "Irrigation Basics," you'll learn how drip emitters, soaker hoses, and timers can help you conserve water. You'll learn about grouping plants by their water needs and minimizing useless monocultures like lawns.

In Chapter 7, "Detective Work: Outsmarting the Pests," you'll learn how to appreciate the good bugs who eat the bad insects in your yard. You'll start looking at your garden as a fascinating lesson in ecology and a fun science experiment. Not as a soldier randomly attacking ant-size creatures who have been on earth millions of years before us, with an arsenal of chemical warfare.

1
Let's Start with a Plan

Let me start by coming clean. I am hereby confessing that when I was an amateur gardener some years ago, I went on plenty of impetuous shopping sprees at my local nursery and planted too many different types of plants in my yard. Instead of looking like a *Sunset Magazine* cover, my front yard looked like something between a second-rate parade, the last day at Burning Man, and a migraine. Shopping at the garden shop without careful forethought and planning sure is instantly gratifying and sometimes emotionally necessary, but too much of this spectator sport will leave you a frustrated, faithless, and broke horticultural failure. Worse yet, word will get out that you have dreadful taste! *Is that really what you want?*

Start small. If you take on too big a garden project, you'll soon be overwhelmed, plants won't thrive, it will look nothing like you imagined, you'll begin to *hate* your sweet hanging birdhouse, your cat, the lawn, the butterflies that were supposed to visit, the leaky tangled garden hose, and you'll give up! Instead, divide your yard up mentally into sections and conquer one at a time. Most plants need critical care at the beginning of their life and then are more independent as they age, which makes the start of a garden the most important period, and the time where you'll have the most to do. Once one area is a success, you can pat yourself on the aching back and move on to the next spot.

If you are a novice gardener with a large yard, I highly recommend you hire a landscape designer to draw you a plan to get started. Prices range from a few hundred dollars to draw up a simple, basic plan to a few thousand dollars for a full-blown computerized design plot of your entire landscape. It's worth every dime because most of us can't see the whole picture in our dreamy, flowery minds. We need the designer/midwife to coach it out of us. You can get local landscape designer recommendations from the staff at your hometown garden nursery. However, if you are inheriting a small- to moderate-size garden and you're up for a fun, long-term challenge, here are some suggestions to get you started down your garden path.

Start by sitting in your yard and not doing a thing. Just sit. Get familiar with the sounds, the scents, and where the sun hits at different times of the day. Then start making a wish list, prioritizing your ideas along with your budget. Look at design photos in horticultural magazines and steal their ideas. I did. Remember, in the garden, there's no greater compliment than plagiarizing someone's work. Talk to other gardeners. Gardeners *love* to talk about plants, almost to a fault. We're like those crazy people you shouldn't approach at the Laundromat. You ask us a simple question and we elucidate till you have to quietly tiptoe away, alarmed by the fanatical look in our eyes as we go on about "heavy feeders," "June drop," and "worm poop."

Another idea is to look for garden tours in your community. Eco-garden tours are becoming more common; gardeners (show-offs) inviting local residents in to come see their sustainable yards. Bring along a camera, paper, and pencil. You can ask the home gardener a plethora of questions. Remember, we're zealots and we love to share our gardening victories. Oftentimes the garden designer, if there was

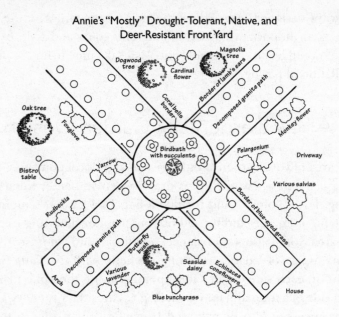

Annie's "Mostly" Drought-Tolerant, Native, and Deer-Resistant Front Yard

My drought-tolerant and mostly native front yard works with Mother Nature, not against her. (Rachel Carson can now rest in peace ...)

one on the home project, is present on the tour day and available for questions as well.

It's also a good idea to start a garden journal. In your journal, you'll sketch your first garden plans. First consider where you'd like to have new planting beds, borders, trees, hedges, or a sunny spot to grow herbs. Perhaps you want to create raised beds for a vegetable garden. Then consider the hardscape features such as paths, ponds, trellises, screens, walls, benches, and paved patios. Maybe you want to add a brick patio or decomposed granite path or to get rid of some of the thirsty lawn. Brick, gravel, or decomposed granite pathways are more environmentally friendly, as they let water percolate through to keep surrounding plants moist instead of running off into the gutter. "Plants come and go, but the pathways are there for decades," says landscape designer Cathy Edger. "Selection of materials for the hard-scape is an important consideration. The color and style of your house should be taken into account. Also, take time to do the proper installation of paving."

A Few Elements of Garden Design

Each area of your garden should have its own focal point—an interesting element where the eye is drawn when you enter the garden setting. Focal points could include a bench, a garden sculpture, a fountain, or an outstanding, tall flowing plant or flowering tree. For each area, you'll also want balance, repetition, and contrast.

One aspect of balance is having elements with the same size or weight on each side of your focal point. Having the same plant on either side of a fountain, for example, gives the area symmetry. Creating balance can also be achieved by giving your garden a theme. Maybe it's butterflies. You may have plants that attract butterflies as well as statues and ornaments that are related to butterflies. Other themes that have shaped noteworthy gardens are choosing one color, for example white flowers, or a Zen garden with water features, or a rock garden with trailing ground covers.

Repetition throughout the garden ties it all together. Repetition or unity is one of the most pivotal factors in making your garden easy on the senses. By creating unity in your design elements, you create harmony and breathing space instead of mayhem. Don't make my earlier mistake and buy one of every plant you fall in love with at the nursery. Not only is that too fickle, you'll get a reputation at the nursery as being "easy." Have a bit more confidence, self-esteem, and self-control and purchase a few (preferably three) each of carefully selected plants that will thrive in your climate zone. You'll want a combination of annual and perennial plants, along with a few shrubs for the background. Although you want unity, you also need to have some plant diversity in order to minimize diseases and attract beneficial insects. In a small yard, you may have 6 to 10 different types of plants and repeat them three times throughout. This will look so much better than a hodgepodge of plants. Trust me. You'll also want to create a low-maintenance garden, so choose a combination of plants that work with the climate and soil conditions of your area. These could be native plants and/or drought-tolerant ones.

Contrast provides variation in your yard through plants with different shapes, textures, and colors. This could mean using two plants of the same size but that have different leaf textures. You'll want a variety of plant forms and flower shapes: round, flat daisy-like flowers; clustered flowers; tall spires; spiky; and flowing.

Color is an important element, too. Cool colors like blue *Myositis* or green *Hosta* recede into the landscape, creating a quieter mood, while hot colors like magenta geraniums come forward and demand attention. You want to create repetition of colors in your planting, too, thereby keeping your color schemes simple. A border where you group flowering herbs such as rosemary, salvia, and scented geranium will bloom with soft, relaxing pastel colors of light blue, lavender, and pale pink.

Last, in your design plan, one of the latest trends in home garden-

---

Annual: A plant that completes its life cycle in 1 year or less.

Perennial: A plant that lives for more than 2 years. Comes back each year for many years.

Biennial: Typically a plant that grows leaves the first year, blooms the next year, and then kicks the bucket on you. (Biennials are less common and you have to wait for a long time to see them actually bloom, so focus on the first two for now.)

---

ing is edible landscaping. Though it may sound new, it's actually ancient. Historically, Persian gardens, medieval monastic gardens, and the nineteenth-century English gardens all combined both edible and ornamental plants. Then in the 1950s the sprawling, water-guzzling, chemical-addicted *lawn* came along and took center stage. In your design, consider removing a section of the lawn and planting ornamental plants along with food-producing plants. Here fruit trees, edible flowers, herbs, and ornamental plants are all beautifully combined, just like Mother Nature originally designed it.

Visiting the Garden Nursery

First, do a little research online, at the library, or in garden magazines to find which plants thrive in your area. You can look up your climate zone in the resource section of this book. Most plant tags at the nursery will list which climate zones a plant will survive in. If you've found photographs of plants you love, research the common name, Latin name, and its growing requirements before you shop. When you head to the nursery, bring your garden journal and take your time. Be honest about whether a certain plant will flourish in your garden, and don't be afraid to ask the nursery staff. Most will be familiar with the local plants and will have a plant encyclopedia on hand. While at the nursery, try to stay focused on what you came for! This can be challenging. Many plants will be crying out and waving their hands, *"Pick me, pick me! Oooh!"* Stick to your guns and choose *only* plants that will thrive in your area. Try to have patience and buy the smaller 4-inch pot instead of the more expensive 1-gallon container full of blooming flowerheads. Purchase the smaller version with only one or two open flowers. This way the plant will use its energy on forming healthy roots in your soil and not on the flowers. Within a few months, that 4-inch plant will have caught up to the 1-gallon size.

Planting

Before planting anything, make sure to read the soil and compost chapters, or the garden gnomes will cross the troll bridge and haunt your dreams. Really. When planting perennials and annuals from the nursery, dig a hole in well-amended soil (where a thick layer of compost has been added on top) to the same depth of the container and a little bit wider. Fill the hole with water and let it soak in. Then fill the hole again and let it drain. Now you're ready to plant. This will help prevent wilting and make sure there's proper drainage. Gently remove the plant from the container. It's fine to tip it upside down to get it out.

Keep notes and records in your journal of your garden's progress each year. You'll see which plants survived storms or stressful periods in your life (when you neglected your garden) and which plants kept kicking. Those are the plants you want more of. Keep notes, and as you become a more experienced gardener, you'll learn from your past mistakes. Gardening is always a work in progress, so join the rest of us suckers who keep striving for the "perfect" garden. I'm not sure we'd even recognize it if we achieved it.

FURTHER GARDEN DESIGN BOOKS AND RESOURCES

Anne Lovejoy's Organic Garden Design Book, by Anne Lovejoy (Rodale, 2001)

Association of Professional Landscape Designers (www.apld.com)

Making Gardens Works of Art, by Keeyla Meadows (Sasquatch Books, 2002)

Planting Design, by Piet Oudolf and Noel Kingsbury (Timber Press, 2005)

A Plant Recommendation from the
Dirt Diva Royal Horticultural Society

Nigella damascena
COMMON NAME: love-in-a-mist

This is must for all new gardens because it's easy to grow from a package of seeds directly sown into your soil. This fine, lacy, fast-growing plant is virtually free of disease and pests! Feathery leaves surround each sapphire blue flower, creating a heavenly, misty green haze around each spectacular large seedpod. Also called wild fennel and devil-in-a-bush. This is a frost-hardy fun annual for cottage gardens. Seeds will self-sow easily. Plants will reach between 1 and 2 feet high and will bloom in spring and summer. They make long-lasting cut flowers and the balloon-like seedpods are easily dried for beautiful bouquets. Also comes in shades of pink and white, but blue is the most common.

ORIGIN: north Africa, southern Europe
HARDINESS: Zones 6–10
GROWING REQUIREMENTS: Nutrient-rich, well-drained soil. Regular water. Thrives in full sun but will tolerate partial shade. My pal Charlie gave me a couple of seedpods a few years ago, and every spring more and more burst into bloom. These flowers keep reseeding forever, and they remind me of Charlie and his prolific, stupendous Santa Cruz garden. Me, jealous of one of my best friend's horticultural abilities? Yes. Is that so wrong?

THE UNIVERSAL BOTANICAL
WHAAA–WHAA RATING: 1

2

Decoding Snooty Botanical Names

Why do Mr. and Mrs. Snooty prefer to use Latin names, one may ask? Why do those plant geniuses at the nursery have to speak in tongues? Here's a petite crash course in botanical nomenclature so the rest of us commoners can slowly infiltrate and hold our ground by tossing those pompous, pretentious names back at them like mud. Then we'll see who's crying!

It all began when the eighteenth-century know-it-all Swedish botanist Carl Linnaeus decided to develop a system of naming plants in Latin in his spare time. If you've ever wondered why botanical nomenclature is confusing, it may be because the guy in charge of the system couldn't quite get his own name straight. Today, he's still referred to as Carl Linne, Carl von Linne, Carl Linnaeus, or Carolus Linnaeus. (Pick *one* name already, Mr. Smarty-Pants!) He thought if he used a botanical, or "scientific," name, people all over the world would understand which specific plant was being talked about without having to give a mind-numbing, lengthy description of each flower. He chose the Latin language because it was, at the time, the international language of scholars. Scientists could then communicate in one big (snooty) language.

In 1753, Carl, stringent control freak that he was, published his book called *Species Plantarum of 1753*. Everyone loved his new system of using the Latin two-word names we presently use, and his paperback went straight to the Amazon bestseller list. Today all plants are categorized methodically by their scientific or botanical name in the International Code of Botanical Nomenclature. Latin is still the primary language, but sometimes, just to beat us down, Greek is used as well.

Here's how it works.

Every single known plant in the world has only *one* scientific name. Using that name will mean there is no confusion at the plant nursery. You'll get what you want. However, any plant can have *many* common names. Common names are like nicknames that your family or friends gave you, and they are different all over the world. They can be pleasant or degrading and affect the plant's self-esteem for its entire life cycle. Some noteworthy, real examples of plant common names are bastard balm, hairy beardtongue, red-hot poker, forget-me-not, jack-in-the-pulpit, blue dicks, and rose turtlehead.

Each scientific name will have two parts. The first one is always capitalized and is the name of the genus, or the generic name. The genus is a group of plants that share at least one characteristic. Think of it as the last name of the family. The second part is the species, or specific name. (Each genus can have several species, often hundreds.) The species name is like a person's first name. The species is always written after the genus in lower case, and both words are properly italicized. On plant tags, however, it is common for only the species name to be in italics. For example, this is how a nursery tag may read at your garden center for the genus *Echinacea* and the species *purpurea*. Tag reads: "Echinacea *purpurea* or E. *pupurea* Common name: Purple coneflower."

The tag may also give the plant's whole family. For instance, "Asteraceae" is the name for the *entire* daisy family. On a nursery tag, this name will be capitalized: ASTERACEAE. Asteraceae is one of the three largest flowering plant families. It contains more than 1,500 genera and 22,000 species.

Stick with me. Nature isn't a neat freak, so it doesn't fit into every single category we want to shove it into, unfortunately. So, to make our heads spin, plants can be further classified into subspecies, varieties, cultivars, and hybrids. A subspecies is a group of plants that is different from others of the same species. This difference may occur in certain geographical areas, such as near a particular mountain, where the flowers are more magenta than the main pink species. A variety also differs from the group maybe by having naturally variegated leaves, but there is no geographical distinction. You'll see the abbreviation "var." after the species name.

Cultivar is a modern term. (The word combines *cultivated* and *variety*.) Cultivars have characteristics that are usually artificially created by propagating plants. The cultivar name is indicated by single quotation marks and follows the genus and species (*Ceanothus gloriosus* 'Anchor Bay'). You'll sometimes see the abbreviation "cv." (Gardeners often use the terms *cultivar* and *variety* synonymously, which confuses us even more.)

A hybrid is a plant that has come from two different species, varieties, or cultivars and has been crossed together. The "×" after the genus name indicates the plant is a hybrid. For example, *Magnolia* × *loebneri*. This is a cross between a *Magnolia* and a *Magnolia stellata*.

What is so sensible about this system is that it is truly universal; a gardener in Japan and a gardener in New York can be looking at the exact same plant, if accurately labeled. Kind of brings a tear to the eye, doesn't it?

Why does any of this matter? Well, first off, you can impress your friends and, well, isn't that reason enough? It also comes in handy when you fall head over heels in love with a plant you saw in someone else's garden and you must have it. Last, and probably most important, is when you know which family a plant comes from, you'll know where to find the information on the conditions necessary to help it flourish in your yard.

Stamens and Pistils Gone Wild

Now that you've learned how to speak Latin (and slam-dunk the show-offs at the plant nursery), it would behoove you to learn a little bit about botany. Understanding how your plants breathe, drink, eat, and reproduce will help you become a more compassionate, respectful, and patient gardener.

Last I heard, the earth is about 4.5 billion years old. For millions of years it was supposedly lifeless; what a waste of time. Then one day a single-celled bacteria called *Cyanobacteria* evolved from other trendy life forms that were popping up at a snail's pace back then. These cells were able to take in carbon dioxide and water and then convert them into sugar and oxygen. In time (millions more years), plants on Earth diversified and evolved into lush tropical rain forests, changing the thick soup of chemicals in the atmosphere to an oxygen-happy planet. Let's recap: If plants weren't here handing out free oxygen, purifying the air, and making food and medicine, we self-absorbed, gluttonous humans would be doomed.

In case you thought flowers were just another pretty face, they are, but they're much more than that. They're the sexual organs of plants, and their main role is to produce seeds. Many of those seeds become flowering blossoms that swell into mature ovaries or fruit such as oranges, apples, or tomatoes so humankind can survive.

THE PARTS OF A PLANT

Leaves

Photosynthesis is carried out by the plant's leaves, which take sunlight, carbon dioxide, and water to create carbohydrates and oxygen. Small openings on the leaves, called stomata, transport water vapor and gases. The stomata absorb carbon dioxide (CO_2) and release oxygen (O_2).

Roots

The plant's very own plumbing system is in its roots. They bring water and minerals up to the stem.

Xylem and Phloem

The xylem in a plant's stem transports water and minerals from the roots upward, whereas the phloem carries carbohydrates generated from the leaves down throughout the plant.

Corolla and Stamen

The corolla is the ring of true flower petals, and inside is where the stamen (male sexual organ) sits.

Filament and Anther

In the flower, the filament is the male stalk that holds up the enlarged anther (finally, some dirty talk) containing pollen.

Pistil

Farther in the corolla of the flower is the female sexual organ called the pistil. It has three sections: stigma, style, and the ovary (which ultimately becomes a fruit).

Pollen

The pollen is the dust-like particles on the anthers of a flower that contain male sex cells.

POLLINATION AND FERTILIZATION

Pollen may come from the same plant to fertilize the ovary (self-pollination) or from a different plant (cross-pollination). Most plants are cross-pollinated and produce separate male and female flowers. These plants depend on wind and pollinators—insects (especially bees), bats, birds, and even gardeners—to help distribute pollen between ripe blossoms. As the pollinator takes in the nectar from the flower, pollen from the flower's anthers gets stuck on the insect's furry body and is taken to another flower, where it's dropped into the stigma. These oblivious pollinators are merely stopping by for a nectar break, similar to a Starbucks run. Each ovule in the ovary must then be fertilized by a separate pollen grain. When pollination and fertilization occur, the ovary swells to form a fruit, the ovules develop into seeds and produce more plants, and the cycle continues.

Want to help the pollinators in your very own backyard? Join the Great Sunflower Project at www.greatsunflower.org, where you can become a citizen scientist collecting local data on honeybees.

A Plant Recommendation from the
Dirt Diva Royal Horticultural Society

Romneya coulteri
COMMON NAME: Matilija poppy or tree poppy

These tall perennials are tricky to get established in your yard, but if you're patient, it will be well worth it and then they may even become invasive. They take their sweet time before they bloom and may sit around in your yard for a year acting all stubborn with nice foliage but no flower. That's okay. We still like them a lot. Their blue-green woody base grows slowly to 6 feet tall and shoots out huge white poppy-like flowers with fluffy golden stamens, resembling fried eggs. This is a spectacular California native plant that I am madly in love with.

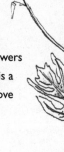

ORIGIN: Unite States
HARDINESS: Zones 7–10
GROWING REQUIREMENTS: Plant in a sunny spot with well-drained soil. Drought tolerant. Cut to the ground in the fall.

THE UNIVERSAL BOTANICAL
WHAAA–WHAA RATING: **2**

3
Tooling Around

Gardening can be hard physical work but also enjoyable and, dare I say, addicting, if you have the right tools. You might even join us gardening buffs someday and bore your friends and family to tears with digital photo albums of your flowerbeds emailed seasonally. Not that *I* do that . . . too often. The right tool will let you enjoy gardening instead of forcing you to quit early, all frustrated and sweaty and saying bad things about me to your neighbors and family. The right tool will help you be more efficient in your garden tasks and yard maintenance. Once purchased, these tools, with a little care, can last for many years, so always choose quality over quantity.

You will require a few good hand tools and that's it. When it's time to shop, if you have an experienced gardener in your life, drag him along, so you don't feel overwhelmed at the nursery. (Don't feel bad. If he's a faithful fan of the flower, like yours truly, he'll jump at the invitation.) Most home gardeners won't need heavy-duty, high-powered, or expensive tools. Should you need something like a rototiller to dig up a large area of a new yard, you can always rent one. I've listed only the most basic tools. You can purchase them over time, so don't feel that you must go out and buy every one of them today. If your space and budget are limited, I'd start with gloves, a hand trowel, a shovel or spade, and a pair of pruners.

And once you get home and start digging . . . always wear sunscreen, a hat, and have a bottle of water nearby. Pace yourself in the yard. Work for an hour or two and then stop for the day or take a rest before you start working again. I don't want to hear how I made you work so hard with your new shovel that you were limping around afterward. Have someone with an inkling of sanity tell you to come inside and take a break.

Essentials

SHOVEL

You can buy a long- or short-handled shovel, depending on what you feel most comfortable with. You'll be using this for moving material, scooping up compost and mulch, or spreading manure and natural fertilizers.

GARDEN SPADE

Generally, a spade has a sharper or more pointed blade than a shovel and is good for digging planting holes, slicing under sod, and digging in packed soil. (If your budget doesn't allow for both a shovel and a spade, I'd choose the spade, but it's nice to have both because one will usually be lost in the yard somewhere . . .)

HAND TROWEL

A trowel is indispensable. You'll use it to plant bulbs, seedlings, and other plants in a garden bed. Try holding a few in the store and see which feels best in your hand. Always return your trowel to the same place each time you use it because it's easy to lose in your garden, where you'll find it rusted out a year later. More and more light-weight and ergonomic styles are now becoming available, some with a rounded handle for more gripping area and less wrist strain while providing more digging power. If your budget allows, have a few of these around.

PITCHFORK (OFTEN CALLED A SPADING FORK)

You'll feel like one of the Beverly Hillbillies the minute you pick up a pitchfork—and that's okay. Get your Jethro on! Whether you're preparing a bed for planting, turning compost, dividing perennials, or aerating a lawn, you will come to love your spading fork. A fork loosens and aerates the soil more than your shovel or spade. It is a must if you're going to have a compost pile. You'll need to turn the organic matter in your compost pile frequently, and a pitchfork will make this workout easier on your back.

RAKE

A steel rake is good for dressing and smoothing out prepared soil in a planting bed. I use my plastic, flexible rake in November to collect all the leaves down my street for mulch. The neighbors may think I'm crazy, but I think *they* are. Leaves are a great source of carbon to add to the compost pile or to leave in your garden to decompose on their own. Having one wide plastic rake for leaves and a small steel rake for soil would be ideal.

HAND PRUNER

A hand pruner's sharp blades allow you to cut thin branches and stems. You will be using your hand pruner constantly, so keep it in a safe, dry place, and go for the best. I've had my Felco No. 2 for the last 10 years, and it's still going strong. The Swiss manufacturer has them in many different sizes, and some are more ergonomic than others. Corona also makes an excellent hand pruner at a more affordable price.

LOPPERS
Loppers are long-handled pruners. They easily cut thick stems and branches. Loppers will make you look and feel super strong.

SCUFFLE HOE
Every gardener should have a scuffle hoe. It has a horizontal blade on the end of a long wooden handle for cutting weeds just below the surface, and it will make hand weeding less tedious.

(Two other handy weeding tools are the three-pronged cultivator and the CobraHead precision weeder. Both of these are shaped like a claw and are superb for loosening soil and attacking weeds.)

SAFETY GLASSES
Wear safety glasses while pruning, chopping, or tilling your little jungle or when spraying your plants. Some models are designed to fit over prescription eyeglasses. This way you can look doubly nerdy.

GLOVES
Get your gloves on! Or your fingernails will look like mine, and that's not very ladylike. I recommend having three pairs and keeping them in three different dry, accessible locations. Choose leather or thick cloth, especially if you will be working around thorns. You may need to replace them annually, as they do tear from overworking. I wear the fashionable paisley gloves from Womanswork (www.womanswork.com).

WHEELBARROWS AND CARTS

You will use your garden cart constantly for hauling materials around the garden or as a container in which to mix soil amendments. Some two-wheeled carts made with pneumatic tires can support up to 500 pounds, though the cart itself is lightweight. I especially like the carts and wheelbarrows available at Gardener's Supply Company (www.gardeners.com) and Lee Valley Tools (www.leevalley.com).

A Few Safety Tips

LEAF BLOWER

Running a leaf blower for a half hour generates as much pollution as driving a car 110 miles. And get this: 80 smart U.S. cities have banned them. Enough with the noise and air pollution! Instead, pick up a *rake*. Rake your leaves around your garden as free fertilizer and mulch. Added benefit: burning calories.

TREE PRUNING

Don't let me catch you up on a ladder pruning the upper branches of your colossal fruit trees. Always use long-handled pruners especially made for tree pruning. If you don't have them, go borrow them from a friend.

REALLY WEAR SAFETY GEAR

I know it can easily look like a fashion faux pas, but you really must wear those gloves, goggles, and a painter's paper air mask if you're going to be spraying products in your yard. Though many are organic, there are still substances in them that could cause harm or, at the very least, dehydrate you. Wash up well after.

Care of Tools

It's almost impossible to store your garden tools correctly 100 percent of the time, but aim for a 70 percent success rate, and they'll last for years. Store them in a shed or other space that's dry and has light, so that they don't rust. You could take an old garden rake, remove the handle, turn it upside down and mount it up in your garage or shed wall. Then hang your garden tools from it. Another good idea is to paint the wooden part of all your tools a bright color so that if you leave them outside in the yard, you can easily find them.

In a perfect world, gardeners should clean tools after each use. Hello, sounds like someone needs a life. . . . Clean your tools as often as possible, though, because the longer soil is allowed to sit on metal, the more rust can develop. If you really want to score an A on your tool test, place a bucket of sharp builder's sand in the shed, and work the metal part of each tool back and forth a bit before you hang it in the shed to rest. At the end of each season it's good to clean all of the metal parts of your tools with an oily rag. This is also a good time to sharpen your blades. You can use a file or a whetstone, found at your local nursery. If you're not sure how to do this, take tools to a professional or make friends with someone who does. That's what I do. Carefully picking and choosing your friends is truly a lost art.

Clematis
COMMON NAME: Virgin's bower, traveler's joy

There are over 200 species of this spectacular woody climber, which is actually quite easy to grow, though it looks more complicated. That's always what we strive for. These showy bell-shaped, flattish flowers are followed by masses of fluffy white seed heads in the fall and winter. At the nursery, you may pay a bit more for a clematis plant, but it's worth it. They're usually trouble-free and long-lasting, and the blossoms are stunning. Two types that fair well in shade are 'Hagley Hybrid' and 'Comptesse de Bouchard'.

ORIGIN: Japan and China
HARDINESS: Zones 4–9
GROWING REQUIREMENTS: Amend your soil with compost to hold moisture, and plant the roots of clematis in the shade but allow the vine to grow up into the sun. If the roots are in the sun, make sure to add a thick layer of mulch. They prefer more alkaline soil, pH 7–7.5. Most require moderate water and are rarely bothered by pests or disease, though a few are more prone to a fungus called clematis wilt. You'll be pruning once a year on these, usually in the early spring. The plant may look quite dead when it's dormant in the winter, but fear not, it will be back with a vengeance the next summer. (Keep the tag name so you can look up if you'll be pruning it in late summer or early spring.) Some varieties like 'Jackmanii', 'Crimson Star', and 'Lady Betty Balfour' need a severe pruning to their ankles, whereas others like 'Henryi', 'Nelly Moser', and 'Ruby Glow' require just a simple thinning.

THE UNIVERSAL BOTANICAL
WHAAA–WHAA RATING: **3**

4

Talking Dirty

IT ALL BEGINS WITH YOUR SOIL

"*Dirt* is the stuff that your nosey next door neighbor likes to dig up on you. Dirt is not, however, emphasis on NOT, a growth medium for plants," palpably elucidates my soil scientist pal, Professor Stephen Andrews, at the University of California Berkeley. "That is the domain of *soil.* Soil, unlike dirt, is a treasure. It matters. And it *should* matter to everyone."

Soil is the backbone of your garden. Nothing else really matters. Don't even waste your time planting if you're not going to first pay attention and admiration to your soil. I've tried. It's like talking to a wall or a garden gate. Nothing changes. Nothing grows. It's just whine, whine, whining you'll hear from your plants, *"I'm hungry, I'm thirsty, I'm tired, I'm bored. Hey, lady, what are you, blind? . . . I'm dying over here!"*

One gram of healthy soil may contain as many as 4 billion bacteria, 1 million fungi, 20 million actinomycetes, and 300,000 algae. Your soil is alive. So quit treating it like dirt.

Soil is a living part of your garden's ecosystem and is the key to successful gardening. Organic gardeners don't feed the plants. They feed the soil and let the *soil* feed the plants. In other words, organic gardeners pass the work onto the underground organisms, and then they can sit around drinking coffee and surfing the net. (If you're good at delegating, you'll be awesome at organic gardening!)

Your soil is full of minerals, organic matter, air spaces, water, insects, and microorganisms. These soil organisms help store and then release essential nutrients to your plants. Your mission, should you choose to accept it, is to keep the underground living system thriving. These soil organisms (mites, beetles, millipedes, earthworms, bacteria, and fungi) power Mother Nature's perfect decay cycle by recycling organic matter (leaves, stems) and turning it into humus (or compost), an end product that your plants can easily digest and is full of nutrients to fuel their growth and development. You may even be voted parent of the year by your plants. This is so much less taxing work than vying for parent of the year with real live children. Finally, we can all feel like winners. Mazel tov!

In soil, size matters.

Scientists classify soil according to the size of the mineral particles it contains then divide it into three categories: sand, silt, and clay.

Sand has the largest particles, which are visible to the naked eye. Sandy soil drains well and has good aeration, but doesn't hold moisture and/or store nutrients well.

Silt particles are fine and feel like powder. Because these particles are slippery when wet, plants have a hard time rooting in them.

Clay particles are the finest of the three. They stick together and can be molded into shapes. Clay dries hard as rock, making it difficult for water and plant roots to break through.

Here in the United States, most of us have sandy or clay soil, but what we all yearn for is *loam*. Loam is a hearty combination of clay, sand, and silt. Loamy soil will hold nutrients and allow water and roots to pass through. That's what you want. You want your soil to invite water, plant roots, decomposers, and nutrients to come for the meal and stay for the pie. Adding compost to your soil will make the loam dream come true. Compost will improve your soil's structure, but you also want to know what your soil's pH level is.

The pH People

Before you plan your garden, test the pH level of your soil. The term pH stands for "Potenz hydrogen" or the potential to be hydrogen. The activity of hydrogen ions in a solution determines the acidity or alkalinity of the solution. The chemist who invented the pH scale actually developed it to test the acid content of his beer!

Most vegetables and flowers thrive in soil with a neutral pH level, somewhere between 6.0 and 7.0. Levels higher than 7.0 are considered alkaline, and levels lower than 7.0 are considered acidic. If the pH is too low or high, plants can't absorb critical nutrients. (However, some plants like azaleas and rhododendrons prefer an acid soil.) A good soil test will tell you the pH level and also which nutrients are present in your soil and in what amount.

The best time to test your soil is in the spring or fall, since extreme weather can skew pH readings. For a rough analysis, you can buy a home test kit available at your local garden nursery. Don't get the $6 variety. If possible, go for the $20 soil test, which will be more accurate and thorough. SoilMaster and LaMotte both make reputable testers and are available online or at garden centers.

If you have a large yard, a city garden, a new yard, or an old one that isn't performing well, you may want to collect a few samples from different areas of your garden and send them to a company that specializes in soil testing. (For soil testing companies, see "The Diva's Little Black (Green) Book.") This can cost $50 to $200, depending on which tests you're requesting.

When doing a soil test at home or by mail, vegetable and flower sections of your yard can be mixed together. (A lawn area should be tested separately.) When digging for specimens, remove mulch and twigs. Don't save the first shovelful from the topsoil. Take the second shovelful farther down. Do this in a few sections of your flower and vegetable garden and then mix the soil samples together in a clean bucket. Then spread the mixed batch onto a clean baking pan and let it air dry for a few hours before testing it.

To lower your pH level (soil is too alkaline), add sulfur. To raise your pH level (soil is too acidic), add lime (calcium carbonate). Your soil tester kit will tell you how much to add. Both of these additions are commonly available at garden nurseries.

Organic Matter

If you have neither the time nor the desire to add amendments in order to change your soil's pH, you can simply add organic matter such as compost to bring your soil closer to a more neutral pH. In fact, the single best thing you can do for your soil is to add organic matter. Your loam dream will come true. This will open up tight soil, help retain moisture and nutrients, improve drainage, and allow air in. It will also attract and feed all those necessary microorganisms that keep your garden soil working for you. As the soil microbes break down the organic matter, they convert it into nutrients that are readily available to your plants over a long time. Through this release of compounds, the soil structure is improved and you have a better chance of growing stress-free plants, which in turn require less water, fertilizer, or pesticides.

- If you add organic matter to sandy soils, you won't have to water as frequently.
- If you add organic matter to silty soil, the soil will be less slippery and allow more air to the roots.
- If you add organic matter to clay soils, your soil will become easier to work and will allow root systems to develop and water to soak in more readily.

Compost, Compost, Compost

My first choice for organic matter is compost. As you will soon discover, I am a compost groupie. I use compost for almost everything and that's all I do. If you don't have time to make your own compost pile (see Chapter 5), you can buy it in bulk at a landscape supply store or bagged at your local nursery. Many community waste management sites are finally doing the right thing and making compost from their community's food scraps. This is certainly the way of the future.

Borrow a friend's truck, or call me and I'll lend you mine. Fill up a cubic yard of compost from your landscape supply company, your local landfill, or your community's recycling center. Gather some friends and have them help you spread it over your yard. Then go over to their yard and do the same. (Keep telling yourself you're having fun!)

Old-school thinking is to dig fresh compost deep into the soil, but I go along with the trendy soil scientists who say "don't dig deep." First, because it is scientifically researched, and second, because it's less work. Too much digging, plowing, and walking on soil only compacts it more while allowing air and sunlight in to the weed seeds. It's best to minimize soil disruption, so instead of digging in fresh compost, just add a layer to the top of your soil and walk away. Do this at least twice a year—in the fall and in the early spring—and add a fresh layer of mulch on top. If you can commit to doing this just two weekends a year (fall and spring), you won't be committing horticultural homicide and constantly buying new plants to replace the ones that bit the dust. Your garden will thrive *and* you won't be standing around constantly spraying dangerous pesticides, wondering why all your plants look cataleptic. Spraying toxic chemicals is so 60 years ago! It went out with those silent, smiling mothers on Valium who held babies in one hand and a cigarette and a cocktail in the other, swaggering around their suburban lawns that had just been sprayed by the ChemLawn guy.

TO DIG OR NOT TO DIG?

If this is a brand-new garden or city plot and you have a sneaky suspicion that the last homeowner just grew weeds, you'll want to remove the weeds and dig in your first load of compost 1 to 3 feet into the soil. But that's only for new yards that you know haven't been worked at all and the soil appears compacted and neglected. After that you can join the rest of us slackers and add a 2- or 3-inch layer of compost to the top of the soil twice a year. (Roughly 1 cubic yard of compost will cover a 150-square-foot area at a depth of 2 inches.) If your soil is hard clay, you may want to buy gypsum to add with the compost to loosen it up and let water flow through. Never add sand to loosen your clay soil. You'll end up with a substance similar to concrete or worse, and I can't bear to see you cry.

In the past, gardeners used peat moss to tighten up sandy soil so it could hold on to water and nutrients. Well, those days are over. We overstayed our welcome (once again), destroying increasingly rare bog habitats by harvesting peat moss. Use compost instead. Compost is a renewable resource. We will never run out of leftovers!

Feeding Your Plants

By enriching your soil with amendments (organic matter), you can decide to fertilize during the growing season or not at all. The necessary raw materials that feed the plant naturally come from nutritious soil. If you have good loamy soil, you won't need to fertilize unless you have container plants or you're growing food. Choose an organic fertilizer. These products are made of natural materials filled with plant nutrients that slowly release over a long period of time at a rate your plants can use without waste. Synthetic fertilizers are usually compounds made in factories, which promote constant bloom and exhaust the plants. The tired plants are then more susceptible to disease and pests. Then you're on the vicious fertilizer and pesticide cycle, which is polluting our local air, soil, and waterways. (See Chapter 8 for more on fertilizing.)

Mulch

While compost is a soil amendment and fertilizer, mulch is a natural weed block. Once you amend your soil and plant your garden, add mulch to the top of the soil around your plants to keep them warm in the winter and cool in the summer. You'll want to add new mulch to your yard at least once a year. You can do this any time of year. I usually add a layer of compost and mulch at the same time, in the spring and again in the fall. Mulch will save you time in your garden because it will eliminate some of the weeding by blocking the sunlight to weed seeds. Organic mulches will slowly decompose, adding nutrients and encouraging our pal the earthworm to stay. Add a 2- to 4-inch layer of mulch to cover the soil surrounding your plants in

HOW MUCH?

How much mulch should you add? Here's a handy little helper:

1 cubic yard will cover roughly 350 square feet at 1 inch deep or 162 square feet at 2 inches deep or 108 square feet at 3 inches deep.

You'll want to have your mulch between 2 and 4 inches deep. Most compost or mulching material costs less than $20 a cubic yard.

---

flowerbeds and all around your yard. (When mulching around trees, keep the mulch a few inches away from the tree's trunk so you don't invite diseases or pests.)

ORGANIC MULCH CHOICES

Decorative Bark and Wood Chips

Wood chips and shavings are excellent mulches. They moderately control weeds and decompose slowly. They should be replaced every few years. Decorative or shredded bark is usually a mix of white fir or pine. Sizes vary between ¼ and 2 inches and most turn gray with age. You can contact a local tree service to ask for free wood chips. There is concern about diseased trees, but most fungi that attack a living tree won't survive on dead wood. Fungi are somewhat choosey about what they attack, but I would ask the arborist about the health of the tree anyway. If the tree was diseased, take the wood chips only if they have been composted.

Cocoa Hulls

Cocoa hulls look awesome, and the chocolate scent is scrumptious! You can add a thin 1-inch layer. Cocoa hulls absorb the heat, are a good weed controller, break down slowly, and add nitrogen to soil. They're expensive, so choose for small areas only.

Pine Needle Mulches

Pine needle mulch is a good insulator in summer and winter and allows water and oxygen into the soil easily. This is a good mulch for acid-loving plants. Spread 3 inches deep around evergreens, strawberries, azaleas, and hydrangeas.

Partially Composted Leaves

Though the appearance isn't very attractive, the insulating and nutrient value of partially composted leaves in summer and winter is excellent. It's best to put a 1-inch layer around plants and add a layer of wood chips on top.

Straw and Hay Mulches

Both straw and hay are long-lasting insulators, but choose straw because hay has too many wayward weed seeds. Straw is good as a cold-weather winter mulch that nourishes and aerates the soil below by decomposition.

Compost, Newspaper, Grass Clippings, Leaves, and Yard Prunings

When you mow your lawn, leave the grass clippings on the lawn or use them as mulch in flowerbeds and vegetable beds. You can also chop up plant cuttings with a lawn mower and spread them around your yard. Soft materials decompose quickly so they're good for flower and vegetable beds, while larger woody cuttings decompose slower, making them better choices for pathways. Thick layers of newspaper make an inexpensive mulch, and the soy it's printed with these days is safe to use. It may last only one or two years though before it decomposes, and you'll need something to hold it down, like a thin layer of shredded bark. The earthworms love newspaper and will call it home.

INORGANIC MULCH
Landscape Fabric

Landscape fabric acts as a blanket you'll place on the soil to block weeds from growing. Choose the fabric over the black plastic options so more air can get in. You'd use landscape fabric in an area of your yard where you don't want to plant seeds or food and simply don't want to work too hard in that section. Maybe you simply want some low-maintenance ground covers to make that area look attractive. (See Chapter 12 for more on ground covers.)

Purchase a large roll of gardener's fabric and cover your amended soil, topped with a wood chip, sawdust, or shredded bark mulch. Cut holes into the fabric wherever you want to place a plant.

A PLANT RECOMMENDATION FROM THE
DIRT DIVA ROYAL HORTICULTURAL SOCIETY

Plumbago auriculata

COMMON NAME: blue plumbago, Cape plumbago

If you need a fast-growing shrub to fill up an area that you don't
have time to pamper, plumbago is your ticket to paradise.
You barely water it, barely tend to it, and barely know
it exists till it blooms and all it wants to do is please
you. It understands that it's all about
you. This evergreen shrub can grow
to 6 feet tall and 8 feet wide, but
it's easy to prune it neatly to a
smaller size, which is what I do in my
yard. Throughout the late summer you'll
be gifted with delicate phlox-like clusters
of light blue flowers on top of graceful arching
branches.

ORIGIN: South Africa

HARDINESS: best in warm climates, Zones 9–12

GROWING REQUIREMENTS: Sun or light shade. Enrich
the soil a bit with organic matter when first planting and
then sit back and be amazed. They can handle a good amount of heat and drought, but
for best flower display, water regularly in the summer. Prune lightly in the late winter
to encourage new growth.

THE UNIVERSAL BOTANICAL
WHAAA-WHAA RATING: **2**

5
Going Compostal!

When I first moved to the West Coast from New York City, I thought anyone having a special bucket in their kitchen to collect food scraps was *whacked out*. I didn't give a thought or actually care where our trash went because, well, I was a New Yorker. Then I met my future husband, Bill, one of those *whacked-out* California environmentalists. He somehow succeeded in transforming me into a proselytizing compost queen. A few years ago we even went so far as to retrieve out of his sister's Dumpster pile "the elite compost tumbler" that she was ready

Close to 40 percent of our landfills are filled with compostable materials that are in return producing methane, a gas 24 times more potent than carbon dioxide and the second-leading greenhouse gas emitted in the United States. According to the Environmental Protection Agency (EPA), landfill methane emissions are the largest source of anthropogenic (human-related) methane emissions in the nation.

to dispose of. There we were driving home on a sunny Sunday morning, with the leaky, muddy, army green compost-spinner rolling around in the back of our pick-up truck. We were in the cab laughing and singing the theme from *Green Acres* as if we had just scored a free flat-screen color TV!

Why Compost?

As we all know, but choose to forget, our landfills are filling up at an alarming rate. Composting is a responsible and efficient way to help the environment, your neighborhood, and your garden. Instead of disposing of things like grass clippings, leaves, and kitchen waste, you'll instead be conserving the plant nutrients they contain. Not only does it allow you to return something to tired, generous, patient, and underpaid Mother Earth but you're also creating a high-quality fertilizer full of valuable soil additives to improve your home garden. You'll save money by eliminating the need to purchase fertilizers because compost has exactly what plants need: water, air, nutrients, and bulk, the last being something most fertilizers lack. Compost improves your soil texture and structure, supplies and helps retain nutrients, provides moisture and aeration, helps control weeds, and reduces the need to buy expensive fertilizers and pesticides that are usually packaged in plastic and adding to more pollution.

Where to Store It?

A simple pile in a corner of your yard will do fine, but a compost container speeds up decomposition and helps repel visiting rodents and their clan. A circular pile made of chicken wire is easy to turn but is not animal resistant. Wood, plastic, cinder blocks, bricks or concrete all make a more permanent structure that'll retain moisture and let in air. The simplest compost bin, commonly found at garden centers, is made of plastic and has a lid that lifts off so you can put yard waste into it and turn it with a pitchfork or shovel. These are fine and good for beginners, but if you become more serious about composting, you may want to invest in a compost bin with stacks or slats that can be removed, allowing access from any side. You'll need to turn your compost pile on a consistent basis, so having access options is great on your back. Prices vary from $50 for a simple beginner model to $500 for the more intricate compost tumbler. Check with your local nursery to see what type of compost bins they have in stock or see "Resources for Shopping, Learning, Community, and Inspiration." Some recycling centers offer compost bins at a reduced price. Check also with your town's waste and refuse department.

What Goes into a Compost Pile?

Place your compost operation site near the house so it's not a hassle to carry out kitchen scraps every few days. If possible, put it in a

A common compost bin made of wood and wire.

slightly shady area so the summer sun doesn't dry it out. Start your pile right on the ground on top of your existing soil. Some common compostable materials are grass clippings; branches; flowers; leaves; chicken, horse, and turkey manure (any herbivores); straw; and kitchen scraps, including conventional or organic fruit and vegetable peelings, eggshells, coffee grounds, and tea bags. *Never* add dairy products, grease, meat, fish, or bones because they're difficult to break down and attract unwanted pests. And never compost anything that has been treated with a chemical pesticide or herbicide. A good way to remember what to add is to do what the garden divas at Green Gulch Farm and Zen Center in northern California taught me: Farm Girls Must Sing! *F* is for "food." *G* is for "greens." *M* is for "manure." *S* is for "straw." Layer and sing like this, and just maybe your yard will become as spectacular and prolific as theirs. They also do a lot of Buddhist meditation on the property. I'm quite certain this continued practice of compassion and peace gets them extra help from above, while the rest of us suffer in our jam-packed-full-of-judgment minds. Fair? You decide.

Keep a sealed container in your kitchen where you collect food scraps. I use a stainless-steel pot with a cover and place it under the kitchen sink. Once or twice a week, bring the kitchen container out to the compost pile. When you add food scraps, try to bury them in the middle of the pile to avoid attracting pests.

BACTERIA AND FUNGI: YOUR NEW BEST FRIENDS

Fungi and bacteria are the microorganisms that control decomposition in your pile. They require both carbon and nitrogen to do their work. Your new best friends love brown and green food. Aim to mix in two-thirds high-carbon materials to one-third high-nitrogen materials. If that's too much to think about, try to simply mix in a relatively equal amount of each, along with adequate air and moisture. High-carbon materials are referred to as "brown." These include branches, sawdust, dried plants, fallen leaves, newspaper, shredded paper, paper toweling, and straw. Materials that have a high nitrogen content, or "green" matter, heat up the pile. These include grass clippings, kitchen scraps, coffee and tea grounds, animal manure, fallen fruit, and fresh plant leaves and stems.

The smaller the materials, the quicker the bacteria will get to work, so take the time, when you can, to cut branches into 6-inch pieces or less. If you are highly motivated, you could also pile up some dry leaves and softer yard trimmings and run them over with your lawn mower. Add those in. When you first start your compost pile, begin by adding layers of compost materials almost to the top, trying to alternate equal greens and browns, then drive a stake into the middle to add air and water. In no time at all, the earthworms in your ZIP code, and their entourage, will be making their way underground to your compost pile. Like a bunch of hooligans, they'll digest your yard scraps with their beetle and millipede friends. There's always a wild garden party going on in a compost pile! Always somebody wondering if they look fat or if they wore the right outfit.

TURNING THE PILE

Turn the pile with either a shovel or pitchfork. Proper moisture and good air circulation are most important, and easy access to turning the pile is vital or else, *trust me again*, you'll find excuses not to turn the pile. If you turn your pile 2 times a week, it will decompose 10 times faster than a pile never turned. The important thing is to keep your pile as moist as a damp sponge and to stir it as often as possible to keep it aerated. If it's too dry or too wet, the decomposing process will stop or slow down. Working 24/7 to break down your compost pile are macro-organisms, like earthworms, mites, grubs, centipedes, flies, spiders, ants, and beetles, along with their microorganism cronies, bacteria and fungi.

Your finished product may take a few months or many, many months to get to the dark, crumbly consistency of healthy compost, but keep persevering. Creating a productive compost pile takes time. Keep refining it as you go along. It's just like the first pancake you put in the pan. That one looks pathetic, but by the time you're flipping the fourth pancake, all of a sudden you look like you know what you're doing! One day you too will stand there proudly, pitchfork in hand, admiring your glorious fresh creation in front of your city-slicker relatives. For a brief moment they will look at you, worried

WHY WE WORSHIP THE WORM

Synthetic fertilizers acidify the soil, adding unnatural levels of salts, which repel our lovely pal the earthworm while dehydrating your plants. Both earthworms and plants should be on low-sodium diets. "Enough with the salt! I'm bloated already," you will hear them cry if you put your ear to the ground. Earthworms are decomposers, digesting organic waste and releasing the nutrients right back into your soil with their castings. For free! They transport minerals from the subsoil to topsoil as they keep the organic matter of your soil just right for good growth. Because an earthworm's castings can be 10 times as nutritious as the plant debris they feasted on, the more the merrier. It will only make your soil richer and your plants happier. To see how many earthworms you already have, dig a hole 8 to 10 inches deep and about 1 foot wide. Count how many earthworms you see:

> **> 8**: Robust soil
> **3–7**: Moderately healthy
> **≤ 3**: Soil needs improvement

(If your soil is in the last category, read Chapter 4 again and apologize to your three famished earthworms. Time to add another layer of compost.)

and speechless. Then they'll pull out their cell phones and call your mother.

Do You Have the Guts to Have a Worm Bin?

If you live in an apartment or a small home without the space for a compost pile, another composting option is worm composting. It's a bit creepy at first, but once you see the results, it's actually quite fascinating. Contrary to what you may think, there is no odor. A worm bin can be placed under your kitchen sink or in a garage or laundry room.

Earthworms (*Eisenia foetida*) help water and air enter and circulate through soil. As they crawl underground they loosen the soil so plant roots have plenty of oxygen and room to spread. They break down organic matter, such as leaves, into nutrients plants can use. An earthworm's body is 72 percent protein. They secrete slime, which contains nitrogen, one of the most important elements for healthy plants. They eat and dump, and leave behind those precious worm castings, which are pure fertilizer. Their castings are rich in trace minerals, plant nutrients, and plant growth enhancers. These nutrients are readily available to the plants and will never, ever burn your plants. Are you sold yet?

In the late 1800s, British scientist and naturalist Charles Darwin spent nearly 40 years studying earthworms. He then hypothesized that worm castings have growth benefits that can exceed even those of plain compost. Recent horticultural studies found the same results. Alas, Darwin, we hardly knew you. Sometimes, late at night when I can't sleep, I'll write your name on the deck with baby earthworms. *Is that so wrong?*

HOW TO BUILD YOUR VERY OWN WORM BOX

1. Get yourself an opaque 10- to 14-gallon plastic storage bin at least 12 to 16 inches deep, with a tight-fitting lid. Drill a dozen pencil-size holes in the top and sides for ventilation.

2. For bedding material, use newspaper torn lengthwise into 1-inch strips or use your shredded documents that you neglected to show the IRS. No color or glossy paper. Wet the bedding with a garden hose and wring it out so it's like a moist sponge.

3. Buy some red wigglers! You can find red wigglers specifically used for worm bins online or at your local plant nursery. Start with 1 pound. (Eight adult red worms can produce 1,500 babies in 6 months.)

4. Fill your bin with the wet newspaper and two big handfuls of garden soil. Mix it up and gently add the worms in, covering them in the paper. Add a handful of food scraps under the newspaper. Cover the bin and keep it sheltered from heat or cold. You could keep the bin under your sink or in the garage or shed.

5. Feed them fruit, vegetable scraps, coffee grounds, tea bags, eggshells, leaves, grass clippings, yard waste. But no meat or dairy and very little citrus, bread, or greasy foods. You could baby them by chopping up food items into smaller pieces but only if you have the time. This will help them enjoy their meal and expedite their work.

6. Check on them once a week to make sure the bedding is still damp. Don't feed them more food till they finish everything on their plate. They will eventually eat the bedding, so add more as needed.

7. In 3 months you will have rich, crumbly soil-like material. These are worm castings! To harvest, move all of the bedding and castings to one side of the bin. Put fresh bedding and food on the empty side of the bin. Give the worms a few days to move on over to the new side. You can then harvest the old side of the bin. Dig the castings into garden beds or sprinkle them on top of your soil.

For the definitive guide to vermicomposting, read Mary Appelhof's *Worms Eat My Garbage: How to Set Up and Maintain a Worm Composting System* (Flower Press, 2006).

HOW TO MAKE COMPOST TEA

Compost tea is a liquid plant food that you can make from compost or worm castings. It's teeming with beneficial microorganisms that help feed your plants with readily available nutrients.

1. Choose a container—a 5-gallon paint bucket or large trash barrel.
2. Add 1 pound of finished compost or worm castings to a couple gallons of water.
3. Fill the container to the top with water and let it sit for 2 to 5 days, covered. Stir it up a few times gently.
4. Strain the liquid tea with a screen into another bucket.
5. Use the tea to water your plants or pour it into a spray bottle and use as a foliar spray.

You can use the leftover solids to side-dress plants, as well.

EXTRA CREDIT
Mike McGrath's Book of Compost, by Mike McGrath (Sterling, 2006)
The Earth Moved, by Amy Stewart (Algonquin Books, 2005)

Helleborus
COMMON NAME: hellebore

This is a low-growing elegant plant, which blooms in the winter and then on and off throughout the spring in warmer climates and requests very little water. White 2-inch, saucer-shaped flowers that slowly turn pinkish with age appear in groups among evergreen lustrous dark green leaves. Christmas rose (*H. niger*) is the most common and can survive even in Zone 3. Corsican hellebore (*H. lividus* var. *corsicus*) is the most sun- and drought-tolerant species. Hellebores look lovely massed in the shade of trees.

ORIGIN: Europe
HARDINESS: Zones 5–9
GROWING REQUIREMENTS: Part or full shade.
Low water. Plants prefer alkaline soil. Plant with plenty of compost. Cut off old leaves when you see buds appear. Deer resistant. Poisonous.

THE UNIVERSAL BOTANICAL
WHAAA–WHAA RATING: **2**

6

Irrigation Basics

Plants require minerals, light, oxygen, carbon dioxide, and water to grow. Almost 90 percent of a plant is water. The process of photosynthesis (converting light energy into chemical energy) would not be possible without water. Plants transpire, or lose water, through tiny pores in their leaves. We then need to add more water. But how does water magically move up the pipe, sometimes 50 to 100 feet for a large tree, to get to the leaves, you ask? That's crazy talk, right? Water molecules and oxygen atoms, powered by the sun, attach to each other in the xylem vessels and pull each other up the stalk to the leaves. Okay, now that I've used the words *atom*, *xylem*, and *molecule* in the same sentence, we can move on. Basically, without adequate water, plant cells won't enlarge and plants won't grow, no matter how many dirty looks you give them. You could have the best soil in the world, but if there's not enough water, the plant will sit there stunted, playing its Game Boy, ignoring you.

Your choices for watering your garden are hand watering, sprinkler, soaker hose, drip irrigation, and other homemade soaking devices. It pains me to see homeowners watering their plants with a sprinkler.

Sprinklers are good only for watering lawns (and not the pavement!).
If you're using a sprinkler on your perennial bed, as I did back when
I was a novice gardener, you're encouraging plant diseases by wetting
the leaves and inviting the *Weed* family to have a family reunion in your
backyard. Sprinklers also waste water when droplets evaporate on leaf
surfaces and in the air.

Soaker Hose

Hand watering your garden with a hose and a fan-shaped nozzle is
perfectly adequate and a nice way to regularly check on your plants.
I did that for years . . . before I had a baby. Then all of a sudden I had
no time to prance around my yard in a hypnotic daze, admiring my
plants. I had to let my garden become secondary while my sweet baby
boy took all of my attention. It was a difficult choice to make, but
after long deliberation, I thought it would look good on my résumé

to play the part of a "good" mother to my son. I told the plants they were going to have to shape up or ship out, and I bought a soaker hose.

A soaker hose is a long section of rubber hose with tiny holes through which water drips out. You'll attach one end of the soaker hose to your home's exterior water spigot. What's great about a soaker hose is that you can lay it out zigzagging throughout your flowerbed. It can be laid under mulch or even a few inches under the soil and left there all season. I'm a big admirer of the soaker hose. If you are a gardener who doesn't have time or the desire to install a drip system or you have a very small garden, a soaker hose will become your new best friend. Get rid of those other best friends. They're just costing you money and time, meeting for coffee, shopping, processing their issues. Your new best friend, the soaker hose, wants to lighten your load. It knows it's all about *you*.

Drip System

There are parts of my yard that I water by hand, mainly so I can hang in the 'hood with my favorite flowers and potted plants, though most of my yard is now set on a timer with a long, sinuous drip system. You can't go wrong with a drip system, and putting it together, attaching all the parts, is actually fun. (Well, at least for the first 2 hours. After that you'll wish you could afford "people.") A drip system will apply water to the soil through drip emitters at each plant so that water is placed efficiently and slowly into the route zone. Setting up a drip system is a bit more costly and time-consuming than simply laying a soaker hose, but it wastes less water, so it would be my first choice. Drip systems have been estimated to save 40 to 50 percent of your water bill. They work well for vegetable gardens, flowerbeds, shrubs, vines, and even container plants.

What I love about the drip system is that anyone, and I mean anyone, can learn how to put it together. If you played with some form of Tinker Toys as a kid (or adult), you are capable of working with plastic pipe. There are three parts to a drip system: a control head, a transmission system of plastic pipes or tubing, and the emitters. You can find various drip irrigation systems at nurseries and hardware stores.

If you can, look for a store with a knowledgeable customer service staff who can help you. It will save you so much frustration in differentiating between the many tiny irrigation pieces. If this is your first time attempting to buy these parts, bring a friend who has done this before, or you may be mumbling bad words about me and your stupid plants and feel as if your head were about to explode. Before you leave the store, ask a few startup questions to the hardware store clerk

HOW TO WATER YOUR LAWN

The average lawn is doused with 10,000 gallons of water each year. (Not rainfall.) Lawns require about 1 inch of water per week to stay green during the summer, according to www.safelawns.org. A good start to conserve water is to have your grass at least 3 inches in height. This way it has a deeper root system, so it draws moisture from a larger volume of soil. You also want to water deeply and less often. This means keeping your lawn sprinkler on a few minutes longer but turning it on only once or twice a week, preferably between 6:00 and 8:00 a.m. Shallow, frequent waterings cause the grass to produce shallow roots that can't survive the summer heat. Deeper and less frequent watering will also help the grass roots to grow deeper than weeds. Weeds thrive with frequent shallow lawn waterings. Don't be like Grandpa across the street, who waters his lawn every day for five minutes. It's a daily pool party for weed seeds over there!

whom you've trapped in the irrigation aisle so you don't feel daunted by the project when you get home. Once you start, you'll quickly get the hang of it, I promise. Once installed, it's always a good idea to periodically walk around your yard when the drip system is on and make sure there are no clogged emitters or leaks. If you're not up for the drip project or your garden is quite small, stick with the soaker hose.

Automatic Timers

At first I was opposed to the idea of having a timer. I like having control of the watering (and everything else in my life), but soon enough I decided to try it, and now it would be hard to go back to pretimer days. Automatic timers are pretty simple to set up. You can buy a battery-operated one from the hardware store that goes right on top of the hose connector. Or you can get a fancier one that is set up indoors, maybe in your garage, and is electronically connected to your outdoor hose bib and then to your drip and/or soaker hose.

Timers are efficient, but don't just forget about them. They should be checked periodically to see if they're still working. They should be turned off in the winter or when a good rainfall is predicted. Don't become too dependent on your timer. It shouldn't replace you as the parent. It can be a good baby-sitter, but ultimately your garden is *your* responsibility. Good gardening is just like good parenting but much less draining because there's no backtalk or PTA meetings.

WATERING SCHEDULES
Because of different climates, soil types, winds, sunshine levels, temperatures, day lengths, and ages of plants, it's difficult to give everyone a perfect watering schedule, but here are a few standard pointers to get you on your way. The general rule of thumb is to water peren-

nials deeply and irregularly, while watering annuals frequently and shallowly. Watering perennials too often and too shallowly will encourage salt build up, provide optimal conditions for certain diseases, and make your plants super-needy. You can test the soil with a garden trowel or an inexpensive moisture meter. Dig the meter or trowel a few inches into the soil of your perennial bed. Make sure the soil is moist 1 to 2 feet deep. Once you see how deep you're watering and that the plants are thriving, you can adjust your watering system or timer accordingly. Seeds are an exception and should be misted briefly daily.

PRIORITIZING YOUR WATERING DURING DROUGHT CONDITIONS

Trees take in carbon dioxide and release oxygen back in the air. They're filtering our air for us for free, so we want to respect and cherish them. Therefore, in times of drought or an extremely dry summer, always aim to save your trees first. A lawn can go brown in the summer and magically come back in the fall rains, while most perennial plants are easy to replace. However, losing a beautiful tree that helped shade your house and backyard in the hot summer means you may have to wait 10 to 20 years for a newly planted baby tree to reach the size of the original tree.

HOW SHALLOW ARE YOU?

HERE'S A HELPER TO GUIDE YOU ON HOW DEEP TO WATER

Leafy vegetables and annual beds: 6 inches to 1 foot
Small shrubs, perennials, corn, tomatoes: 1 to 2 feet
Large shrubs and trees: 2 to 4 feet

DON'T BE A CHUMP WARNING

WHY ARE WE WASTING ALL THAT RAINWATER?

A 1,000-square-foot roof will yield close to 600 gallons of water from 1 inch of rain. More and more gardeners are placing rain barrels, which are simply large containers, under a downspout from their roof. This is a smart way to stockpile water in areas with wet winters and dry summers. Many models have a spout or a hookup for your hose, or you can simply fill up watering cans from the top, to water your plants when the weather dries up again.

WHEN TO WATER

The best time of day to water your garden is early morning. This allows the least amount of water to be lost to evaporation. It also gives leaves a chance to dry off in case they got wet during the watering session, thus avoiding a possible fungal disease. But mostly, it's an excuse for gardeners to dress like crazy people. This is how it works. I have my timers set for 6 a.m., but there are some plants in pots on the deck that I need to water by hand every few days. So, I go out into my backyard in a sweater, pajama bottoms, and red polka-dotted rubber boots. There, I wander around aimlessly, hand watering flowers, turning the compost pile, talking to our cat, Binkey, and sipping Earl Grey tea. It's the most divine part of my day.

Penstemon
COMMON NAME: beardtongue

You gotta luv the penstemon because it hardly needs water! Most grow to about 3 feet wide by 3 feet tall. This happy native perennial requires little care. Some species are even considered wildflowers. All they ask for is a little sunshine, and they're on their way to pleasing you, blooming from summer to fall. And the color selection is huge! You'll want them all, from deep dark blue to purple to rosy red to magenta to pale white. For colder climates (Zone 3), try *Penstemon digitalis*. This is a frost-hardy native with lavender bell-shaped flowers. 'Husker Red' has gorgeous reddish purple foliage with pink flowers and attracts hummingbirds. Palmer's penstemon is a West Coast drought-tolerant native with purple flowered stalks up to 8 feet.

ORIGIN: United States
HARDINESS: Many varieties can survive in Zones 3–10.
GROWING REQUIREMENTS: All thrive in full sun and require little water or care. In the hottest climates, they can stand partial shade. Don't overfeed or overwater these plants, or they'll die on you. Good drainage is necessary, but the soil doesn't have to be too rich. They'll do best in rock-garden conditions.

THE UNIVERSAL BOTANICAL
WHAAA–WHAA RATING: **2**

7

Detective Work

OUTSMARTING THE PESTS

A healthy garden is home to a variety of native and flowering plants, which in turn attract a wide variety of beneficial insects who enjoy lunching on the neighborhood pests. How do we invite beneficial insects and a bunch of their friends to come to our homes to eat and hang out like starving teenagers? To start, reduce or eliminate all broad-spectrum pesticides, herbicides, and fungicides. Pesticides eliminate not only the bad insects, but kill the beneficial ones, too. Then the surviving bad bugs are free to take over, surrounded by so few natural enemies. Use of pesticides can also produce insect strains that are resistant to the very same pesticides you're using. As a result, you'd need to purchase even more and stronger bug sprays. You're now on an endless cycle of wasting money; weakening your plants; killing off the bird, butterfly, and bee populations; depleting your soil; and polluting the neighborhood's groundwater. That's not gardening. That's *lunacy*!

Many of the key ingredients in pesticides were created during World War II as agents of chemical warfare. (The term *pesticide* is used for insecticides, fungicides, miticides, bactericides, and herbicides.)

Many were designed to disrupt the central nervous systems of its prey, be it mosquito or human. After the war, the pesticide industry met its true love, the advertising industry. They formed a marriage made in heaven for them and in hell for home gardeners. Together, they promise you the perfect yard while understating the inherent and very real health dangers and risks. Today, these very same multibillion-dollar industries continue developing poisons for use in agriculture, forestry, fisheries, home gardening, and lawn care.

"All pesticides are toxic to some degree . . . and most pesticides have not been adequately tested to determine their effects on people or the environment," according to the EPA's website. Where do these caustic chemicals go after you've sprayed them? They evaporate and drift upward or they trickle and leach into the local water systems. If you're not using them, your next-door neighbors probably are. They may be pumping systemic insecticides into their ground, which will soon leach over to your side of the fence whether you have an "Organic Zone" sign up or not. Your used-to-be-organic garden is toast, baby! But, the problem doesn't end there.

Pesticides can be absorbed into the body through the skin, eyes, and lungs. Most can cause instant flu-like symptoms or long-term diseases. When asked, many homeowners admitted they didn't even read the directions on the product packaging, so they're oftentimes spraying more than what's necessary and not wearing protective gear. "New scientific studies are finding that pesticides can damage the human nervous system in ways we haven't understood before," says Kristin Schafer, associate director for advocacy with Pesticide Action Network. "Children and the elderly are especially vulnerable, with both autism and Parkinson's increasingly linked to pesticide exposure."

In 1998, the Science and Environmental Health Network gathered a group of scientists, philosophers, lawyers, and environmental advocates at the Johnson Foundation Wingspread Conference Center in Wisconsin, yielding this concise definition of the moral and political principle called "The Precautionary Principle": "When an activity raises threats of harm to the environment or human health, precautionary measures should be taken even if some cause-and-effect relationships are not fully established scientifically." If we wait for scientific certainty (which takes forever, usually due to lack of funds), damage to humans, animals, and/or nature may be irreversible. For example, when I was growing up in the 1970s, smoking was strongly suspected of causing lung cancer, but it took many years (of lawsuits with tobacco companies) before the link was conclusively demonstrated to the satisfaction of scientific standards. By then, many smokers had died of lung cancer, and all of us kids had been inhaling secondhand smoke as we sat in the backseat of the station wagon without seat belts, eating Twinkies.

"Children are at a greater peril [than are adults] from pesticide exposure because their organs and immune systems are still developing," the EPA states on its website. The National Academy of Sciences estimates 50 percent of lifetime pesticide exposure occurs during the first five years of life.

I'm not a big fan of many insects or of pesticides, but can't we all just get along? Insects have been on earth for over 400 million years. Of the nearly 1 million insect species entomologists have identified, *less than 1 percent* are actually considered pests of agriculture.

The Good Guys

Many insects are pollinators and therefore critical for fruit and seed production. Some insects are also predators and parasitoids and prey on other garden pests. Insects also help break down organic materials in the soil and act as food for other insects, birds, and animals. They are truly model citizens in your yard. A garden filled with a diversity of plants will attract beneficial creatures such as hummingbirds, honeybees, bats, ladybugs, dragonflies, lacewings, and mini-wasps. Most of these visitors crave a bug sandwich for lunch.

Most insect allies perform their best control services and are most useful during their immature stage. However, once they reach the adult stage, these beneficial bugs are productive pollinators, so you want to have plants in your garden that are rich in pollen and nectar. Your goal is to provide the necessary food, water, and shelter to attract a variety of beneficial bugs and to encourage them to take up residence in your yard. Some winning insectary plants (plants that whistle to the good bugs to come on over) are aster, calendula, California poppy, lilac, dill, rosemary, black-eyed Susan, sunflower, yarrow, zinnia, and all native wildflowers. Create a natural habitat by imitating nature. Nature loves a mixed bag! Plant a wide variety of natives, ornamentals, and edible plants that are proven winners in your climate zone, and then let at least a small part of your garden flow wildly and untamed. Trust me, in a home with a perfectly manicured, rigid, and flawless cookie-cutter yard, I doubt anyone is getting lucky (and I don't mean the insects).

Some habitat heroes are the immature lady beetle who feeds on scales, mites, thrips, and the eggs of other insects. One ladybug can devour 5,000 aphids in its short lifetime. One wren can consume more than 500 insect eggs, beetles, and grubs for an after-school snack. Those industrious, yet annoying ants that take over your kitchen countertop a few times each year love to feast on termites, and some can also pollinate plants. They eat organic materials in your compost pile as they aerate and recycle nutrients such as potassium and phosphorous back into your soil. Dragonflies can eat 300 mosquitoes and gnats each day, while spiders can eat their own weight of various garden insects in one meal. Spider populations average around 50,000 in 1 acre of green space, and of the 100,000 species known, only a handful are considered dangerous to humans. Wolf spiders pursue their prey by chasing them down and giving them the old stare-down scare tactic. Having keen eyesight and swiftness, they hang out in the subterranean world of our backyard soil and then pop out to feast on crickets, earwigs, ants, sow bugs, and beetles. Bees get more bang for their buzz when there are lots of flowers to visit and pollinate in just one small area. Recent studies show that many bees prefer native plants over exotic ornamentals, so again, stick with your local habitat.

Though worldwide honeybee health has been on the decline since the 1980s, it wasn't until the fall of 2006 that beekeepers nationwide began noticing honeybee colonies disappearing in large numbers without known reason. This syndrome is called colony collapse disorder or CCD.

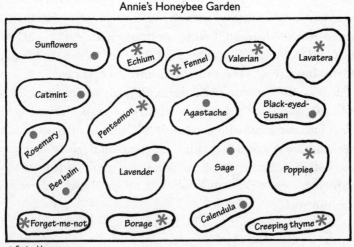

Annie's Honeybee Garden

* Spring bloomers
• Summer bloomers

Have three to five of each plant for maximum nectar production and pollination for a long time. Most of these plants prefer a sunny location.

Honeybees (*Apis mellifera*) are *polylectic*, which means they feed on just about anything that's blooming. Besides gathering nectar to produce honey, honeybees pollinate home gardens, orchards, wildlife habitat, and especially agricultural crops. We need them if we want to have food in the future, so plant flowers that the queen bee and her worker bees like to visit: agastache, borage, bergamot, black-eyed Susan, buckwheat, calendula, catmint, California poppy, catnip, *Clarkia*, coffeeberry, coneflower, coreopsis, cosmos, *Echium*, forget-me-not, gaillardia, lavender, penstemon, *Phacelia*, rosemary, salvia, scabiosa, sunflower, tansy, tidytips, verbena, and wild lilac.

You're the Decider

It's time to put on your thinking cap and learn about integrated pest management (IPM). The IPM program began when commercial growers became concerned with the high costs, pest resistance, and health concerns associated with synthetic pesticides. Soon homeowners and pet lovers began looking for safer ways to manage pest problems instead of going straight for the insect spray.

IPM allows us to monitor and deal with pest problems in a way that will ultimately lead to longer-lasting control of pests while using fewer and less harmful pesticides or none at all. IPM is a decision-making process. *You* are the decider! This is how you will begin to look at your yard's pest and disease problems. There are four parts to IPM: cultural, physical, biological, and chemical. Mix and match these as you patrol your turf.

CULTURAL (EMPHASIZES PREVENTION)
When growing fruits and vegetables, choose disease-resistant plant varieties.

Always choose plants for the correct area of your yard—for example, sun or shade.

Avoid infected seed, plants, soil, or containers.

Use sterile planting mix and clean containers for indoor seed starts.

Improve your soil at least annually. (Say "Compost and mulch" three times and mean it!)

Eliminate pest hiding places by cleaning up debris.

Practice organic lawn care so your lawn isn't a weed hangout.

Rotate vegetable crops each year.

PHYSICAL (EMPHASIZES THINKING AND LABOR)

Handpick pests and place in boiling water. Step on snails. (Apologize later.)

Spray pest with a strong spray of water from a garden hose before considering an insecticide. (This works extremely well on aphids.)

Remove diseased plants as soon as possible. Toss in garbage.

Use caulk to plug holes in buildings.

Add weed-control fabric to new planting areas to help deter weeds.

Use traps, food baits, netting, fencing, tree bands, and copper barriers.

Hand pull weeds. (Or have your people do it. Who wants to bend so much?)

Get out the battery fly swatter. Fire it up!

BIOLOGICAL (EMPHASIZES ENLISTING OTHERS)

Encourage natural predators by avoiding broad-spectrum pesticides and providing water, food, and shelter for the good bugs.

Plant nectar-filled plants that will attract beneficial bugs. (Good Bug Blend is one such seed mix; available from www.groworganic.com.)

Buy beneficial bugs online.

LEAST TOXIC CHEMICAL CONTROL (EMPHASIZES SPRAYING AND PRAYING)
Last-Resort Option

Use mineral oil or vegetable oil sprays on fruit trees.

Choose a product for a specific pest.

Use less toxic products like soap sprays and botanical pesticides derived from plants.

Some Less Toxic Product Options to Control Pests

The products discussed in this section are all commonly found at nurseries and will break down into harmless compounds in a few days. It's always best to take an insect specimen or a diseased leaf to your local garden nursery or Master Gardener desk to get a true diagnosis before purchasing any products. You can get some help identifying a certain pest in your yard at the National Gardening Association's fantastic website (www.garden.org). Search in their Pest Control Library under *Bug Mugs*.

SOAP SPRAYS

Soap sprays work wonders for soft-bodied insects such as aphids, mealy bugs, spider mites, spittle bugs, and stink bugs by dehydrating them. Mix 5 tablespoons of dish soap (or insecticidal soap from your nursery) into a gallon of water and spray directly on the leaves. In the spring, when aphids are all over your precious roses, you may have to repeat this spray twice, about a week apart. Spray early in the morning so rose leaves can dry off in the sun.

BACILLUS THURINGIENSIS (BT)

Bacillus thuringiensis, or Bt, as we in the biz call it, is a naturally occurring bacterium that destroys many leaf-chewing caterpillars and is even safe to spray on crops. Works best on small caterpillars and works fastest when it's exposed to sun. It works slowly, so be patient. It's safe to use around mammals and beneficial insects and is very specific to the target pest. However, it may kill butterflies as well, so use only as a last resort. Bt can be found at most garden nurseries.

PYRETHRUM

Pyrethrum is derived from crushed chrysanthemum blossoms. It harms specific insects such as aphids, small caterpillars, flea beetles, and other chewing and sucking culprits. It doesn't affect humans and is biodegradable, but it is moderately toxic to some mammals. It isn't safe for fish and can be a threat to water quality, so don't use this one if you live next to a creek. Apply it in the late afternoon or evening and not when any bees are around. Use pyrethrum only as a last resort.

DON'T BE A CHUMP WARNING

Pyrethrum spray is widely available at nurseries. Some pesticide manufacturers are creating synthetic versions of pyrethrum, sometimes called *pyrethroids* or *pyrethrin*, which were designed to replace certain banned pesticides and are not as safe (and making us consumers have to think too hard!). So look at the label to make sure it is organic and plant derived.

NEEM OIL

Derived from the seeds of the native Indian neem tree, neem oil acts as an appetite suppressor and growth inhibitor on cucumber beetles, mealy bugs, and mites. Neem oil is a less toxic broad-spectrum pesticide that also works well as a fungicide and insect repellent. It can be sprayed on plants and trees at intervals, usually in early spring.

Going After the Bigger and Crunchier Pests

SNAILS

Snails are hermaphrodites, so both males and females can reproduce, sometimes birthing 100 eggs at a time. They love to eat your favorite plant leaves. But don't let that scare you. Just step on them and crush them a few inches down into your soil or lawn. They'll help fertilize. Don't toss them over the fence. They come back and they bring their friends.

Copper barrier tape is widely available and can be fastened around planter boxes, wooden frames or tree trunks so that when snails come upon it, it sends a signal through their body somewhat similar to being electrocuted. (Apologize after. Say, "Sorry, my bad.")

You can also collect them at night and put them in a bucket of boiling water. If you don't believe in hurting insects, and you have a sealed compost bin, you could put them in the compost. They'll party in there eating other pests and plants. When you use your compost, you'll have to sift them out with a chicken wire screen.

Cut-off plastic bottles are great for protecting young seedlings from snails. Cover the seedling at night and gently remove the bottle in the morning. Another option is to place eggshells around your plants.

Diatomaceous earth is made from needle-sharp fragments of prehistoric sea creatures and fossils. Spread it around leaves, branches, and the ground. It scrapes and pierces the bellies of snails and slugs. Wear a mask when dispensing it, as it's a powdery, harsh substance that can irritate your lungs. It's considered safe to people and animals.

Products like Sluggo or Escar-Go are both safe around pets, kids, fish, and other wildlife. These are iron phosphate pellets that cause the snails and slugs to stop feeding, although it can take several days for the snails to die.

Always stay away from snail baits with metaldehyde. They're toxic to fish and birds and contribute to hundreds of pet poisonings and deaths per year.

MOLES AND GOPHERS

If you see zigzagging tunnels in your garden, you've probably got moles. They can be helpful by aerating your soil and eating many insects; however, they also eat earthworms. Drop mothballs into the first run to discourage more tunneling.

Try mole and gopher repellent made with castor oil. This can be placed into holes in the grass via a spray or dry granules. Moles and gophers are repelled by castor oil. A product called Mole & Gopher Med is biodegradable and available at many nurseries.

Traps or baits may be necessary if they're reproducing like mad and ruining your lawn. Be vigilant. They're all persistent. Some gardeners flush these guys out of the hole by flooding out their tunnels.

Others have had good results simply pouring a bottle of hot sauce down the hole. Whatever you do, make sure to take a moment to laugh at yourself, standing out there alone on the lawn at 6 a.m., trying to outsmart a gopher.

RODENTS

Set rat traps with baits of peanut butter, banana, or a hot dog. Remove ivy, a favorite hiding place for rats. Break up dense plantings with exposed paths. Most cats will go after mice but not rats. What a bunch of spineless furballs.

Keeping your yard clear of clutter and debris will help keep rats away. Keeping your compost pile tightly covered and placing edible scraps only in the center and pushed far down in the center will also help send rats to someone else's garden. If they're getting out of hand, stop using any food scraps in your compost pile for a few weeks.

RABBITS

Sprinkle pepper on and around young vegetable seedlings or sprinkle blood meal or a product made with fox urine such as Shake Away around your garden in the evening. For trees, place a 2-foot cylindrical fence of chicken wire around the tree. This will also discourage mice. Get a dog and let him guard and do something useful for a change.

DEER

About 80 percent of the average deer's diet is shrub foliage. First apologize to the deer for suburban sprawl right onto her turf. If deer are frequent visitors, and you can't put up a tall fence, then your best option is to plant *only* deer-resistant plants in that area. You'll want to plant shrubs with small leaves that deer find less tasty. It's like feeding them liver and onions. Rosemary, breath-of-heaven, *Grevillea*, butterfly bush, rockrose, and rhododendron are good options. Oleander is one of your best bets for a tall, easy shrub or screen. It produces a chemical called tannin that deer detest. Hellebores are also filled with a toxin that deer despise. They also are not fond of bitter, furry, fuzzy, spiky, and smelly plants. As for deer-proof perennials, try scabiosa, gaillardia, and lamb's ears. Strong-scented plants include lavender, scented geranium, catmint, and salvias.

Garlic Clips are clips you place on your plants every 2 to 4 feet. They're filled with a concentration of garlic oil that is 1,000 times stronger than garlic juice. They last about 6 months and come in packages of 25. (Worth a try for rabbits and deer.)

Another option is Liquid Fence, a spray made with garlic that lasts about a month on leaves, which I've had good results with. (Hold your nose while applying. It really stinks but just for an hour or so.)

Home gardeners should *never* use a Category I pesticide! You'll see the word *poison* on the container along with the word *danger* and a skull and crossbones. These products can kill an adult with less than 1 teaspoon or a few drops of accidental ingestion. Category II pesticides will be labeled *warning*, and Category III and IV will be labeled *caution*. This rating summarizes the immediate or acute toxicity of digesting a product (or sometimes it studies the immediate hazard of absorbing it through the skin), but it does *not* consider the *long-term* health hazards, the ability to cause cancer or birth defects, or the impact on the immune or endocrine system. Home gardeners should use only products labeled *caution* and only as a last resort.

Call 1-800-CLEANUP to find out where to dispose of the pesticides in your shed. Or contact the National Pesticide Information Center at 800-858-PEST. For less toxic product options, see the extensive list of alternatives to combat many common pests at Our Water—Our World (www.ourwaterourworld.org).

Visit the Environmental Working Group (www.ewg.org) to learn more about the Kid-Safe Chemicals Act. It's morally wrong that babies are being born prepolluted with hundreds of toxic industrial chemicals.

EXTRA CREDIT

Visit What's on My Food? (www.whatsonmyfood.org) to see how much pesticide residue is on your store-bought fruits and vegetables. For example, apples showed 42 different pesticides, lettuce had 52, and blueberries came in at 48. These tests were performed by the USDA over the last ten years. They also list the toxicity of each pesticide and the associated health risks. *Solution: Grow your own food, support your local organic farmer, or toss produce in the washing machine with a load of laundry. Air dry and enjoy!*

Tagetes lemmonii
COMMON NAME: mountain marigold, Copper Canyon daisy

This 3- to 5-foot-tall airy-fairy, fern-like shrub has a somewhat sprawling habit, and you either hate the scented leaves or love them. Many insects don't like the smell, so they stay away. When you brush against them, they give off the smell of marigold, mint, and lemon. They'll bloom in late summer with many bright orange daisy-type flowers. Tagetes will bloom in the winter here in California when nothing else too exciting is happening in the yard. It really is a trouble-free plant.

ORIGIN: Arizona and Mexico
HARDINESS: fairs best in Zones 9–11
GROWING REQUIREMENTS: Full sun and moderate water.

THE UNIVERSAL BOTANICAL
WHAAA–WHAA RATING: **3**

PART TWO

Growing Your Garden

There's no one style or absolute right way to garden, and gardeners globally are proving that. Small flower and vegetable gardens are sprouting up on rooftops, apartment terraces, front stoops, in downtown parks, schools, abandoned lots, and even organically on a section of the White House lawn. Victory gardens and community gardens are making a comeback as well. Move over, Agribusiness—there's a new sheriff in town. In this part, I cover different types of gardens, such as urban and native gardens, and show why trees should be a part of your long-term landscape planning no matter where you garden. Trees purify our air, absorb pollutants, and release oxygen, all without asking much from us.

In Chapter 8, "Garden Rehab: How to Fertilize Naturally," you'll learn an important lesson about fertilizing: Feed the soil, not the plant. When you feed the soil, its microorganisms work around the clock feeding and nourishing your plants. You finally will have your own people.

They'll just be a little invisible and . . . *creepy*.

In Chapter 10, "Going Native and Loving It," you'll learn how much less maintenance and water native plants require. Their flowers also attract insect allies to your yard that will eat pests for lunch. All for free!

Chapter 12, "Ground Covers: Who Ya Gonna Call," denounces large lawns. Lawns are yesterday's news! They've milked enough water, chemicals, and cash out of us, and now it's time for them to go away. Get ahead of that toxic train wreck and learn about planting low-growing ground covers as lawn alternatives, especially if you live in the West or Southwest, where rain seems to be taking a long siesta.

In Chapter 13, "Shall Hell Be Paved with Weeds?" I tried to find a few positive things to share about weeds. That hurt my brain. So, instead I offer less toxic herbicides to use such as corn gluten meal, acetic acid (vinegar), and herbicidal soaps, along with a playlist for you to listen to on your iPod while you're out there on your hands and knees, pulling weeds, sweating, and mumbling about I how I told you hand-weeding burns calories and can be therapeutic. *Can we still be friends?*

8
Garden Rehab

HOW TO FERTILIZE NATURALLY

Giving Your Garden a Clean Start

Unfortunately, many unknowing gardeners feed their plants with a mined, salty, chemical, fast-acting fertilizer that can deplete the soil, burn young seedlings and earthworms to a crisp, and turn your plants into speed-junkies. You don't want hyperactive and sugar-addicted plants. (Aren't hyperactive and sugar-addicted children enough?) Stop being an enabler.

Synthetic (chemical) fertilizers may give you a prolific flower and vegetable garden for a few weeks, but in the long run they actually weaken your soil. Chemical fertilizers don't improve soil structure or feed the earth. They leave your plants poorly nourished. If you continue down that rocky road, your soil will, year after year, degrade into a subsoil-like medium that is less and less conducive to root growth. Trust me, again. The first few years of my gardening life was just that. I had no idea what I was doing and thought purchasing the colorful container of fertilizer on sale at the check-out counter was going to make my garden bloom-happy. It did, for a few weeks, and then everything wilted or got a disease, and I saw insect infestations that made me literally run screaming through my yard. So, I did what every novice gardener does. Fed them more, more, more fertilizer. Slowly the plants shriveled into alien-looking fossils. In the garden business we refer to this syndrome as "horticultural homicide."

Most synthetic fertilizers contain only nitrogen, phosphorus, and potassium and rarely contain secondary nutrients that plants are craving, such as calcium and magnesium. Chemical fertilizers also dissolve quickly into the soil. If it should rain soon after or you've just watered, these chemicals get transported deeply into the earth, where they're useless to your plants. This is called "leaching." The chemicals have gone so low down that they're merely polluting your neighborhood's groundwater.

Sobering Up

Organic fertilizers are natural, slow-release fertilizers. They take their sweet time steadily releasing their nutrient content and supporting the complex ecology of microorganisms in the soil. They're made from animal, mineral, or plant material usually minimally processed if it all. Since I've been adding thick layers of compost to my yard twice a year and growing cover crops each fall, I rarely purchase any fertilizer at all. The cover crops I plant in the fall, along with the compost I add, work to break down nutrients slowly, having a longer and safer effect than fast-acting chemicals. If I fertilize at all, I make my own compost tea, which is teeming with beneficial microorganisms, and feed or spray the plants in the spring and summer. *(Do I sound like Martha Stewart? I still don't know how to make my own water.)*

DON'T BE A CHUMP WARNING

Do a little research before purchasing and don't support gardening companies who have been polluting the planet for the last 60 years and all of a sudden are selling green products just because organic is now the hottest-selling sector of the gardening industry. What a bunch of phonies! Here are a few organic gardening companies I trust, who, at their core, have had a clean and green business philosophy before it was way-too-late, trendy, and profitable to be environmentally responsible: Arbico Organics, E. B. Stone, Foxfarm Soil & Fertilizer, Flower Pharm, Dr. Earth, Gardens Alive, Gardener's Supply Company, Peaceful Valley Farm Supply, Spray-N-Grow, TerraCycle, and Whitney Farms.

But let's say your soil (and your compost pile) is still young and isn't filled with the magnificent microbial activity that well-amended soil has, and you're having a backyard party later in the summer and have to impress your relatives with your gardening proficiency. You may want to purchase an organic fertilizer.

How to Read a Fertilizer Label

On all fertilizer containers you will see the letters *NPK*. Those letters and numbers tell you how much nitrogen (N), phosphorus (P), and potassium (K) is in the fertilizer. These are the three most important nutrient elements of the 17 necessary elements for plant growth and development. For example, a bag of fertilizer labeled as 5-10-12 means it contains 5 percent nitrogen, 10 percent phosphorus, 12 percent potassium; the rest is inert filler.

Introducing the Primary Plant Nutrients

Element	Function	Organic Sources
Nitrogen (N)	Gives plants their dark green color; stimulates rapid growth	Blood meal, fish emulsion, manures, worm castings, cottonseed meal
Phosphorus (P)	Stimulates root formation; gives new plants a good start; critical in formation of seed	Rock phosphate, bat guano, bonemeal
Potassium (K)	Increases resistance to disease; stimulates strong, stiff stalks; promotes sugar, starch, and oil production; improves quality of crop yield	Seaweed, greensand, granite dust

Introducing the Secondary Nutrients and Micronutrients*

Element	Signs of Deficiency†
Magnesium	Discoloration of leaves, interveinal chlorosis
Calcium	Plant's growth stopped, blossom-end rot
Sulfur	Light green to yellow on young leaves
Zinc	Thin, yellow leaves; low yields
Iron	Yellowing of leaves (but veins are green)
Copper	Stunted growth, wilting
Manganese	Stunted growth, chlorosis of young leaves
Molybdenum	Symptoms vary
Boron	Boron
Chlorine	Wilting, followed by chlorosis
Nickel	Leaf tip death

Above are 14 of the 17 essential plant nutrients; carbon, hydrogen, and oxygen are the final 3.

*Add sparingly to help address deficiencies in your soil.

†If the leaves on a certain plant are showing unhealthy symptoms, take a sample to your local garden nursery or Master Gardener desk to get a better diagnosis.

What You'll Find at the Nursery

Many minerals, soil amendments, and fertilizers are available in large amounts at landscape supply stores and garden nurseries. The real *plant nurseries*, not garden centers in the huge chain stores, will be more knowledgeable about these additions. You may want to purchase a mixed formula or one with a specific supplement—for example, one high in nitrogen. On the packaging you'll find the correct amount to use and what the best time is to add it in.

Some Common Organic Fertilizers

In the following lists, the average NPK ratio is given in parentheses.

ORGANIC SOURCES OF NITROGEN

ALFALFA MEAL (5-1-2) is high in nitrogen, vitamins, and minerals and is a good activator for soil organisms to get to work converting nutrients into an available form at a moderately fast pace. Alfalfa meal is a great soil amendment, especially for newly planted roses, but it is good for all plants. This is also a nice side-dressing for vegetable crops, especially corn, which is a heavy feeder.

BAT GUANO (8-4-2) is straight from the butts of bats and is full of *fast*, readily available nitrogen, phosphorus, and many trace minerals.

DON'T BE A CHUMP WARNING

Always wear gloves when adding fertilizer, handling animal manure, or working around your compost pile.

BLOOD MEAL (11-3-0) is really dried blood from animals. The soil organisms turn it into readily available nitrogen.

COFFEE GROUNDS (2-0.3-0.2) are easy to come by. They know me at my local Peet's Coffee, where I can collect 50 pounds of coffee grounds in a day! Coffee grounds don't belong in the landfill. They belong tossed right on top of our soil. They're excellent for lemon trees and even roses. You can add your morning coffee grounds and tea bags to your compost. I recently met one of the horticulturists from Prince Charles's organic garden at Highgrove. They spread out their tea bags from their afternoon tea around their favorite acid-loving plants. If the Brits do it, that officially makes it the proper thing to do.

EARTHWORM CASTINGS (1-0-0) are created from nonsmelly worm poop and are high in organic matter and supply a plethora of trace minerals.

FISH MEAL OR EMULSION (7-3-0) is a natural organic fertilizer made from fish or fish by-products containing important trace elements. It works quickly and is filled with nitrogen and some phosphorus. (Note that it is seriously stinky for the first few hours.)

MANURE (HORSE, CHICKEN, TURKEY, DUCK, RABBIT, SHEEP, COW) is best used when aged or sitting around in a heap for a few months, not straight out of the pooper-shooter. You can mix it into your compost pile to help break it down more rapidly or let your own separate pile age for 3 to 6 months before using it in your garden. All are relatively high in nitrogen and bacteria, with some having more phosphorus and potassium than others. Ask your local stables, zoo, or neighbors if you can come by to lighten their load of animal poop. They'll be thrilled. Ask them if their animals have been treated with medications or if the manure pile has been sprayed with pesticides. These chemicals can suppress microbial populations in compost, so you may want to go find your free, uncontaminated animal turds elsewhere.

SOYBEAN AND COTTONSEED MEAL (7-2-1) are relatively fast-working high-nitrogen fertilizers. You can purchase them inexpensively at animal feed stores. Ask if they contain GMOs or pesticide residue. If so, go with alfalfa meal.

ORGANIC SOURCES OF PHOSPHORUS

BONE MEAL(3.5-15-0) is derived from highly ground bone and is high in phosphorus and calcium. It works slowly, so it's safe for new plantings and can help in transplant shock. Bone meal also promotes good root systems and is an all-around excellent plant food for more blooms.

ROCK PHOSPHATE (VARIES) is long lasting but slow acting. It's also filled with calcium and many trace minerals and can increase root activity in transplants and seedlings. Soft-rock phosphate, also called colloidal phosphate, may contain less phosphorus but is in a form that plants can more easily use; it breaks down slowly in the soil for years.

ORGANIC SOURCES OF POTASSIUM

KELP MEAL (1.0-0.8-2.5) is made from dried seaweed harvested from the ocean. Kelp maintains a high content of plant growth hormones and regulators, essential trace minerals, and organic material that is released slowly and acts like plant vitamins. It will increase the health of roots and the plant. It is useful as a foliar spray in the hot summer on stressed plants. Kelp and fish emulsion are nice combined.

GREENSAND (0-1-8) is an expensive mineral powder that is a slow-release source of potassium. I don't have much experience with it, but many gardeners love it for improving the structure of clay soil. It contains 32 trace minerals.

WOOD ASH (0-2-6) can be used to raise the pH of your soil instead of using lime. This might be a good choice if you heat your house with wood. The ash is high in calcium. Use it sparingly and don't put this in your compost pile because it can kill off many of the good microbes. It's also very alkaline, so don't use it around acid-loving plants.

Remember, you are not alone in your garden-detox efforts. The Dirt Diva has your back. I promise, once you get your garden sober, you will never go back to a life of enabling chemical dependency. The most exciting thing for your plants to look forward to sniffing in your new drug-free garden may be some fresh cocoa-hull mulch or organic coffee grounds. Rock on, clean and sober. Caffeinate and dominate!

GENERAL FERTILIZER: PLANT SNACK

For a monthly plant booster during the growing season, here's a snack for your plants that you can mix up at home. Most of the ingredients you can purchase in bulk from a farm feed shop or a plant nursery. Mix up a batch in a metal container or a large trash can with a top and keep it in a shed away from pests and rain. Rake this in when you're planning a new garden bed or as a side-dressing (feed around the plant's drip line) for existing flowers and vegetable crops.

Ingredients

3 parts soy or cottonseed or alfalfa meal (nitrogen)

1 part rock phosphate or bonemeal (phosphorus)

½ part kelp meal (potassium)

This powdered mix is concentrated, so don't overfeed. A 6-inch pot requires just 1 tablespoon, a gallon-size plant requires ¼ cup, a large shrub could use 1 cup, and a tree will love 1 to 2 cups at the drip line.

A PLANT RECOMMENDATION FROM THE
DIRT DIVA ROYAL HORTICULTURAL SOCIETY

Tithonia rotundifolia
COMMON NAME: Mexican sunflower

This is one of my favorite annuals. It's a vigorous, 5-foot-tall plant with large velvety leaves and 3-inch orange-red dahlia-like blossoms cranking out all summer long. Plant in the back of an annual border. It may need some staking if it's windy. Try *T. diversifolia* if you have room for a 15-foot-tall perennial with yellow flowers in Zones 9–11. *Tithonia* makes an excellent cut flower and attracts Monarch butterflies and bees.

ORIGIN: Mexico and Central America
HARDINESS: Zones 4–10
GROWING REQUIREMENTS: Thrives in sun and warm temperatures in light, well-draining soil. Don't overwater them! They're tolerant of drought and don't want pampering or fertilizer. Deadhead regularly, and you'll have more flowers. Keep water off of the leaves, as the plant can be prone to fungus.

THE UNIVERSAL BOTANICAL
WHAAA-WHAA RATING: **3**

9

The Urban Gardener

Greening our cities isn't happening only in the center of the universe, New York City. It's all around us. City dwellers from coast to coast are realizing their personal connection to the land, the farmers, their food, and the planet. Rooftop gardens, community gardens, and farmers markets are spreading across the nation. The buzz is in the air. City slickers want to grow their own organic vegetables on a terrace, or a window box full of herbs, or a barrel of cosmos and daisies right on the front stoop.

Though there's information in this chapter dedicated to small-space gardening, it would behoove you, *Cosmo* reader with the green thumb, to go back to the beginning of the book to learn about the importance of good soil that's teeming with microbial life from the continual addition of compost. The advice throughout the book is for *all* gardeners, whether they're deep in the country or high up in the city. As soil scientist Stephen Andrews says, "The mantra throughout the land should be "Compost, compost, compost. Mulch, mulch, mulch!"

Growing in Containers

If you have space on your terrace or porch, container planting is a good option for you. Clay pots are nice looking but tend to dry out quicker than other planters. If you live in an area that freezes, clay pots can also crack. Plastic pots cost less and, though not as attractive, hold moisture longer. (You can find recycled plastic pots that have been saved from going to the landfill at www.terracycle.net.) Ceramic or other decorative materials are beautiful but are more costly. Wood looks attractive but may last only a few seasons until it starts crumbling apart. Whichever container you choose, make sure it has a drainage hole at the bottom and at least a 12-inch diameter at the top. Anything smaller will require too much watering, and then you'll blame me for your patio failure. Especially you New Yorkers.

Garden soil, used alone, is too dense for containers and also tends to dry out quickly. It's best to purchase a large bag of potting mix, which will be free of disease organisms and weed seeds. Distribute this into containers along with an organic balanced fertilizer at planting time.

WHAT TO PLANT
Trees

If you have the space on your terrace, first plant a tree in a large container. This way you'll have some shade during the hot city summer. Once your tree is established, after two years or so, it'll become very low-maintenance, so trees are always a smart investment. Some trees that can withstand many weather elements and some city pollution, either on your porch or on the street, are the mimosa tree, white birch, dwarf conifers, various maples including Japanese maple, flowering pears, Sargent cherry, crepe myrtle, fig, columnar apples, and lemon trees. (Fruit trees will need to be moved indoors in the winter in Zone 6 and under.)

Flowering Shrubs

City slickers can even grow roses on their rooftops as long as there's 6 hours of sunlight and it's not too windy. Some urban-trained dependable roses that can grow well in tubs, planter boxes, or raised beds are 'Betty Prior', 'Carousel', 'Spartan', and 'Vogue'. Shrubs such as sweet mock orange, forsythia, camellia, azalea, rose of Sharon, smokebush, lilac, and yew are also suitable for urban conditions. Good climbers for a trellis or patio wall are wisteria, English ivy, Virginia creeper, Japanese honeysuckle, *Clematis* 'Blue Boy', morning glory, and creeping myrtle.

Vegetables

If you have a sunny space, you have a good chance at growing vegetables in the middle of your metropolis. Some of the easiest crops for an urban garden are plants that don't take up much space such as lettuce, scallions, and chard and crops that can maximize space by being staked to grow upright, such as cherry tomatoes, beans, and peppers. Just remember that vegetables need care and require constant moisture. In extremely hot weather, vegetables growing in containers may have to be watered twice a day. Be ready to serve.

It's best not to plant edibles in a patch of soil that happens to be down the street, on the sidewalk near your apartment building. If that's your only option, first do a full soil test not only for pH levels but for metals, especially if children will be eating the crops. Mercury, lead, and cadmium levels are ubiquitous in most urban soils from motor vehicle exhaust, lead paint, and other industrial waste. Children's bodies are actively growing and can easily be poisoned from contaminated produce. Always wash crops thoroughly before eating if grown anywhere in the city.

Herbs

Herbs also do well in city container gardens. Some nice combinations for pots are basil, cinnamon thyme, and tarragon or parsley, chives, and oregano. Lavender and many sages look great all by their soothing-scented selves and deserve a pot or two on your deck. Most herbs require sun and minimal water while inviting beneficial insects and repelling certain pests with their strong fragrance.

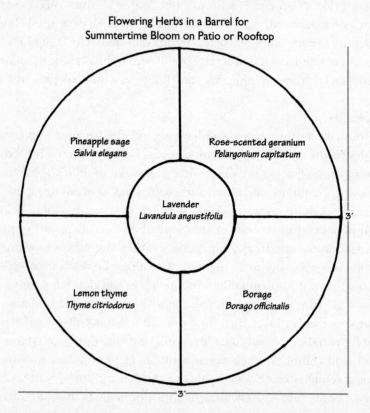

Flowering Herbs in a Barrel for
Summtertime Bloom on Patio or Rooftop

Pineapple sage
Salvia elegans

Rose-scented geranium
Pelargonium capitatum

Lavender
Lavandula angustifolia

3´

Lemon thyme
Thyme citriodorus

Borage
Borago officinalis

3´

If starting with plants, place three to four 1-gallon plants in each section. If planting by seed, use one seed package in each quadrant and thin out.

Some annuals and perennials that have proven themselves to do well in containers:

Alyssum	Marigolds
Begonia	Nasturtium
Boxwood	Pansies
Browallia	Periwinkle
Coleus geraniums	Petunias
Common hydrangea	Salvia
Impatiens	Snapdragons
Lantana	Wallflower
Lobelia	

WHERE TO PLANT
Window Boxes

Catching sight of a building with a window box overflowing with geraniums in the middle of a bustling city just makes my day. A window box is a great option for city dwellers who have no patio, balcony, small plot, or front stoop. The box could be made from plastic, wood, or terra-cotta but must have a drainage hole and must be securely fastened to your window. Choose a window that receives the most sunlight and is closest to a water source, if possible. You'll probably want to stick with annuals here because most of them are not as deeply rooted as perennials. You could buy two to three 6-packs of annuals and divvy them up between two window boxes. For an artistic look, choose three tiers: a trailing foliage plant such as lobelia, ivy geranium, or impatiens; a cascading flowering plant such as fuchsia, petunia, or certain pansies; and some small upright flowers such as marigold or snapdragon. The city air can dry out your window box quickly, so make sure to water often and feed lightly once or twice a month with a balanced fertilizer during the spring and summer.

Hanging Baskets

Hanging baskets look charming on patios, terraces, and front entranceways. They're fun to design but need frequent watering in the summer. For a container, terra-cotta, wire or rattan baskets, metal urns, and wood containers all work well. (You can line a wire basket with a preformed, moss-covered sponge liner or a cocoa fiber liner.) Hang it with chains, wires, or rope. If you use a swivel hook, available at most nurseries, you can turn the plant occasionally so the plant gets light on all sides.

When choosing plants, try to begin with a color scheme. Some color is good, but too many mixed colors can cause your friends to talk about you behind your back. Flower designers like to use "a filler, a thriller, and a spiller." Choose an upright thriller plant in the center (geranium, coleus, ornamental grass), then a few fillers around it (salvia, verbena, licorice plant), and one or two trailing plants (ivy geraniums, lobelia, sweet alyssum).

FERTILIZING CONTAINER PLANTS

When growing plants in the city and containers, there's a good chance the beneficial microbes aren't hanging out in your potting mix doing their magic, so you'll want to fertilize your plants every 2 weeks or so during the growing season. You can simply add a shovelful of compost or a combination of fish and seaweed emulsion, which are full of trace minerals.

Apartment dwellers may not have a place to have a compost bin, but a worm bin under the sink or in a laundry room is very doable. If the worm part bothers you, don't worry. Once you're up and running, you rarely see the worms. They like the dark, so they'll be at the bottom of your worm bin busy eating your leftover food scraps and creating the most nutritious fertilizer for you. If you're up for it, see page 46 on how to make your own worm bin.

WATERING

The first promise city gardeners need to make is "I will water faithfully." Your plants are stuck in the middle of a busy metropolitan area with little greenery or friends or beneficial bugs or normal people around them. They *need* you! So make a long-term commitment to nurture them, especially during the winter cold and summer heat. Never let the soil completely dry out. Okay, put down the book and go water them. I'll wait for you. . . . Hurry up already!

Urban Art

Because of the recent interest in the environment, organics, and more natural style, our outdoor spaces are being transformed into colorful, comfortable, sometimes lavish and spiritual outdoor living spaces. We want our terraces to be an extension of our home's interior. This is nothing new for city slickers who live in small apartments. Outdoor living rooms are common simply because indoor space is so tight. Now it's trendy to have outdoor living rooms.

Recycled materials are also here to stay. Old Victorian doors and old windows can create an airy garden partition for an outside room. Buddha's are in. Aged mirrors, wind chimes, sun-catchers, and whimsical insect tchotchkes are in. Garden gnomes are out. They may seem harmless, but they're actually friends of the devil with those pointy shoes and piercing hats. They want to infiltrate your yard and stalk your cerebral cortex.

A mirror can make your outdoor space look bigger and seem like

ITCHING FOR MORE SPACE TO GROW THAN YOUR WINDOWSILL?

Looking to improve the quality of your life by beautifying your neighborhood, producing food, conserving resources, creating self-reliance, being physically active outdoors, and socializing a bit? Join a community garden! Visit www.communitygarden.org to find a community garden in your 'hood. Here you'll learn about the mission of the American Community Garden Association, a nonprofit organization that works to promote and support all aspects of community food, ornamental gardening, and community greening in urban and rural communities.

you have more flowering plants than you really do. But mirrors can be dangerous to pigeons, so if you hear any crashing on your terrace, you might want to remove the mirror. There's also the slight possibility of a fire from the reflection on a sunny day, so keep mirrors in a shady area. (In case of accidental fire: immediately toss in all gnomes and run for your life before they cook your brain.)

A PLANT RECOMMENDATION FROM THE
DIRT DIVA ROYAL HORTICULTURAL SOCIETY

Echinacea purpurea
COMMON NAME: purple coneflower

Meet the coneheads. They're drought tolerant or at least not heavy drinkers, and they're offspring from a dependable, dramatic, yet happy-go-lucky family, with little obvious dysfunction. What's not to luv? They can easily be grown in pots, and they attract insect allies, honeybees, and butterflies. They're also relatively deer, pest, and disease resistant. Traditionally echinaceas are mauve to pink, but new hybrids have appeared in the last few years with sunnier colors. They're tolerant of hot summers but like to be mulched and kept cozy in the wintertime. They make excellent cut flowers.

ORIGIN: United States
HARDINESS: Zones 3–9
GROWING REQUIREMENTS: Can stand a tad of shade but will have better and bigger blooms in full sun. Moderate to low water. Feed with a balanced organic fertilizer once in midspring and again in midsummer. They reseed easily. Snails can be a problem. Keep an eye out for them and squish them into the soil as added free fertilizer.

THE UNIVERSAL BOTANICAL
WHAAA-WHAA RATING: **3**

10

Going Native and Loving It!

Oftentimes, new homeowners, yours truly included, move into a house with a yard and immediately decide they want to grow roses (mostly hybrids from China or Europe) or fuchsias (from Central America) or impatiens (many from Africa), instead of growing plants that belong in their area. When we stick with our native landscape, we're supporting plant communities that have evolved and survived over thousands of years. Once native plants are established, they carry on without a chirp. Not one complaint. They just want to hang by your side in your yard and make your life easier.

Why Go Native?

To conserve water, time, energy, and money—go native. How's that for motivation? Many native plants are drought tolerant. Drought-tolerant plants, once established, survive on rainfall and little additional watering a few times a month, in the summer. Most native plants even perform better *without* fertilizer, and many are pest resistant and rich in nectar, so they invite birds, butterflies, and beneficial bugs to your side of town. Most need minimal care and need pruning only once a year, usually in the fall before they go dormant. Native plants essentially take care of themselves. They're not needy. They're laid-back, smart, good-looking, and independent. In other words, they're the perfect date.

It's about changing your planting perspective. Once you do that, it will all make sense to you. Old-fashioned and outdated gardening emphasizes selecting exotic plants and planting them in your garden so you can then give them life support: lots of water, feeding, and coaching. If our old ways programmed us to change our landscape to accommodate the plant, growing natives teaches us to select the plant that goes naturally in the place. Repeat three times a day till you're convinced: "Select the plant that goes naturally in the place." You can thank me later.

By planting natives, you'll be inviting not only insect allies to go after the pests but also hummingbirds. Who doesn't ❤ the hummingbird? Hummingbirds must consume half their weight in sugars each day, so they're attracted to flowers that are rich in nectar. They'll feed on nectar but will also consume a tiny insect or two for dessert. Hummingbirds are truly fascinating to watch and exciting to see in your garden. In early spring, the male hummingbird finds a home near a food source, and then finds a mate. Together they line the nest (the size of a walnut), or decorate the pad, in bright colors. The female lays two eggs, each half the size of a jellybean. Eggs incubate for 11 days, then deliver tiny hummingbirds. Some native plants that will invite hummingbirds to your garden are bee balm, hummingbird sage, honeysuckle, coralbells, columbine, lupine, milkweed, and penstemon.

How to Start

If you don't have time or money or energy to take out the old garden or turf, chip away at your yard slowly. Consider making your lawn smaller, a section at a time, or maybe take out a foot or two of the border and start planting natives there. If you live in the west or south, consider desert plantings, while East Coasters can look into woodland plantings of trees, shrubs, and ferns. The folks in the middle can substitute with a low-maintenance prairie-type meadow. Visit the library or look online for information from your local native plant society. There you'll find the most common native plants that are the backbone of a natural habitat in your area. You can also re-create the layers of plants you find in local parks while you're out hiking or mountain biking. (You do that, right? You're not just sitting on the couch watching cable TV? The Home and Garden channel is okay.)

Planting Natives

When planting natives, purchase them in 4-inch or 1-gallon containers at the nursery. Many plant nurseries now have a native plant section. If yours doesn't, ask them to get with the program! When planting, if you've amended your soil in that area with compost regularly, it's not necessary to add a shovelful of compost into the planting hole. No mollycoddling necessary! Just fill the planting hole with water and let it soak down to make sure there is good drainage in that area. If so, go ahead and plant. Then add a 3-inch layer of mulch, such as leaves or wood chips, so the plant thinks it's back home in the wilderness. Keep mulch away from the plant stem.

Water consistently the first year. This is the most important time to keep plants from drying out. By the second or third year, they'll be ready to go on their own. Then you can water them only in late spring and early summer, once or twice a month if there's been no rain.

Native plants can also be grown in containers. You'll want to grow them in a fresh potting mix, not soil, which can be too dense. Some good plant options for containers in the sun are yarrow, verbena, monkey flower, black-eyed Susan, coyote mint, and various sages. Some good shade options are coralbells, columbine, and iris. You could also grow a wildflower seed mix of annuals in a pot. Some happy campers are Chinese houses, farewell-to-spring, poppy, red maids, and tidytips. Top-dress natives growing in containers with a handful of compost later in the season if they're not performing well. During a hot, dry summer, you may have to water more often.

SEASONAL TASKS

Though native plants require much less care than conventional garden plants, you'll need to do a few simple seasonal tasks.

Fall

Cut off the top growth of late-blooming perennials like Matilija poppy and hummingbird sage to encourage new growth.

Dethatch your tall grasses and ferns by running your hands through the clumps and loosening up the old dead leaves. You can also use a rake to do this, or if the plant is large and messy, cut it back to the ground. It will come back.

In most areas, the fall is the best time to plant natives to get them acclimated to their new home. Many nurseries have fall sales.

Winter

In late winter, sow seeds of spring annual and perennial wildflowers.
In late winter, divide perennials.

Also, in late winter, get hold of weeds! Don't shake up the soil too much. This will bring new weeds. Hand pull or gently use your scuffle hoe.

SPRING

Dare I say it? Get a good start on weeds—before they set seed.

Prune out any dead branches lightly to improve air circulation in shrubs or trees.

Top-dress potted plants with compost.

SUMMER

Move pots to a shadier area because they can overheat. Water even the drought-tolerant ones during a hot week.

Cut back spring perennials, like California poppies, to stimulate another succession of bloom.

Water newly planted native seedlings and grasses.

NATIVE PICKS

Here are recommendations of some lovely, widely available U.S. native perennials. Pick and choose according to your climate zone. Check with your local nursery to see which will thrive in your area. To find more local choices, go to PlantNative (www.plantnative.org). For traditional Native American crops and native seeds, visit Native Seeds (www.nativeseeds.org).

Perennials—Sun

BEE BALM (*MONARDA DIDYMA*) Average water, grows 2 to 5 feet with intricate spiky stalks and unusual tubular lavender, pink, or scarlet flowers that attract butterflies and bees. I love this plant! Zones 4–10.

BLACK-EYED SUSAN (*RUDBECKIA HIRTA*) Average water, grows to 3 feet with yellow daisy-like flowers with a dark brown center. Has a wonderfully long bloom time. Keep deadheading for more blooms. Zones 4–9.

BLANKETFLOWER (*GAILLARDIA*) Fast-growing 2- to 4-foot perennial with showy yellow daisy-like flowers with a red ring around a dark orange-purple center. The name blanketflower refers to the yellows, oranges, and reds of some Native American blankets. They tolerate heat, wind, poor soil, cold, and dryness in Zones 5–9.

BLUE VERVAIN (*VERBENA HASTATE*) This tough cookie can even sustain life in New York. Quite frost hardy. Will grow taller than other verbenas and can bloom all summer with pretty small blue flowers. Zones 3–9.

CARDINAL FLOWER (*LOBELIA CARDINALIS*) Average water, grows 3 to 5 feet with unique showy red flowers above a mass of purplish leaves. Zones 2–8.

CONEFLOWER (*ECHINACEA PURPUREA*) Tolerant of drought, grows to 4 feet with purple petals surrounding a dark pincushion-like center. New flowers provide nectar for butterflies while the old flower provides seed for birds. Zones 3–10.

PENSTEMON (*PENSTEMON GLABER*) This woody-based species from Wyo-

Botanical name: *Gaillardia*
Common name: blanketflower

ming grows to 2 feet tall with purple to red tubular flowers with white tips. A late-summer-blooming beauty. Zones 3–10.

SWAMP MILKWEED *(ASCLEPIAS INCARNATA)* Average water, grows to 4 feet with clusters of pink flowers that are a favorite eating spot for Monarch butterflies and their larvae. Zones 3–9.

Perennials—Shade

CORALBELLS *(HEUCHERA SANGUINEA)* Part sun to part shade, low water, super-fast grower. Attractive plants that form a round mound of lobed, textured leaves most of the year with thin stalks of reddish flowers to 2 feet tall in the summer months. This plant asks for so little and is happy to give! Zones 3–8.

LARGE-FLOWERED TRILLIUM *(TRILLIUM GRANDIFLORUM)* Average water, grows 1 to 2 feet tall in slightly acidic soil, with white-pink flowers in erect stalks. Zones 4–7.

TRUE FORGET-ME-NOT *(MYOSOTIS SCORPIODES)* Originated in Europe but is now considered an invasive native in America. This is a perennial version of the sweet annual forget-me-nots and the state flower of Alaska. Tiny blue flowers with yellow centers bloom in woodlands all spring and summer. Zones 5–9.

RED-FLOWERING CURRANT *(RIBES SANGUINEUM)* This gorgeous shrub can grow to 12 feet tall, slowly. Pink flowers appear in the spring with bluish blackberries following in the summer. Flowers attract hummingbirds, while the berries are a food source for other birds. Zones 6–10.

WILD COLUMBINE *(AQUILEGIA CANADENSIS)* Part shade, average water, grows to 3 feet with whimsical red and yellow flowers that attract hummingbirds. Easy to grow. Zones 3–8.

WILD GINGER *(ASARUM CANADENSE)* Average water, grows to 6 inches, and spreads as an evergreen ground cover with glossy heart-shaped leaves. Zones 3–8.

FURTHER NATIVE GARDENING READING

100 Easy-to-Grow Native Plants, by Lorraine Johnson (Firefly Books, 2009)

Designing California Native Gardens, by Glenn Keator and Alrie Middlebrook (University of California Press, 2007)

Bringing Nature Home, by Douglas W. Tallamy (Timber Press, 2009)

TWO NATIVE AND DROUGHT-TOLERANT MAIL-ORDER OPTIONS

High Country Gardens (www.highcountrygardens.com) specializes in gorgeous plants suited for low-water and native gardening.

Annie's Annuals (www.anniesannuals.com) specializes in spectacular, rare, heirloom, and unusual plants, many of which are native and not heavy drinkers.

Warning: Severe drooling can occur when perusing these two catalogs.

A Plant Recommendation from the
Dirt Diva Royal Horticultural Society

Rudbeckia hirta
COMMON NAME: black-eyed Susan

Black-eyed Susans are considered a perennial but are usually grown as an annual. Average height is 2 to 3 feet tall. Carl Linnaeus named *Rudbeckia* after the scientist and botanist Olof Rudbeck, who saved Linnaeus from poverty by hiring him to tutor his three children. At the time, old Linnaeus wasn't selling much of his plant research because the town bishop was in an uproar about the taxonomist's graphic flower pollination theories. Descriptions of pistils and stamens "in the marriage bed" was considered too X-rated for 1808.

ORIGIN: Appalachian highlands
HARDINESS: Zones 3–9
GROWING REQUIREMENTS: Prefers well-drained soil, partial shade to sun, and moderate water. Very resistant to heat. Deadhead frequently. Easily self-sows. This is a deer-resistant plant that attracts butterflies and pollinating bees. You can also find cultivars available in shades of orange and gold. Does superbly as a cut flower.

THE UNIVERSAL BOTANICAL
WHAAA–WHAA RATING: **3**

11

Go Plant a Tree!

J. Sterling Morton, a journalist and the editor of Nebraska's first newspaper, kicked off the original Arbor Day on April 10, 1874. Part journalist and part settlement promoter/politician, Morton realized the expansive rich farmland that Nebraska could provide but that it lacked the necessary wood for building houses or fuel to heat homes. Morton decided to offer prizes to counties and individuals for planting the largest amount of trees. On that very first Arbor Day, more than 1 million trees were planted in Nebraska! Since then, many other states and countries have passed legislation to observe Arbor Day each spring.

Why Become a Tree Hugger?

Not only do trees add grace and beauty to our yards but they provide fruit and berries for jams, jellies, maple syrup, and critical substances used for pharmaceutical and medicinal purposes. They can increase property value and provide shade, which can reduce utility bills from air conditioners. Finally, established trees take in moisture from the air and need little summer watering. Trees are a smart, economical long-term investment. They just stand there silently (some Redwood trees for 3,000 years!) staring at us, rolling their eyes at our arrogance and stupidity, wondering how come it took us so long to figure out we could recycle paper products. Today, it's time to become a tree hugger!

Trees are an important part of your garden design; they create the basic structure and support the smaller landscape plants. And in case you're a hermit, like yours truly, they create a natural screen to obscure the view of your neighbors (and the mufflers and boats on their front lawn). A yard without trees looks bare and uninviting and a little pitiable. There's also the C-word: the carbon factor. According to the U.S. Forest Service, "During a 50-year life span, one tree can generate $30,000 in oxygen, recycle $35,000 worth of water, and clean up $60,000 worth of air pollution."

Before you decide which tree to plant, decide if you want an evergreen tree (has foliage all year long) or a deciduous one (loses its leaves in the fall and winter). Deciduous trees will give you a splash of fall color, a dramatic look of bare branches, sunlight through the branches in the cold winter, and shade in the summer. Evergreen trees have leaves all year long so they can give you shade and privacy all the time. After you've decided which type, deciduous or evergreen, there are hundreds of trees to choose from: ornamental, fruit bearing, dwarf, weeping, vase-shaped, and so on. You'll have to do some research on your own, but first consider which trees are native to your area. Native trees will thrive without much care or water, making you look like a model citizen.

Planting a Tree

Once you've chosen a tree and its planting location, make sure the soil has been tested for its pH. Also make sure the area has been amended recently with a top layer of compost. Check that your chosen location has plenty of space around it for tree roots to grow out and that future mature branches won't hit any overhead wires.

It's time to get your hands dirty and start a profound bond with something so miraculous, charitable, and inherently valuable to mankind: trees. When purchasing trees, buy the small to medium ones. It's economical, and the tree will establish itself quicker than will a large one that has lost more of its roots when it was dug.

You can plant a tree any time, but late fall or early spring, when a tree is dormant, is best.

PLANTING A TREE

1. Choose a site with good drainage and the appropriate sunlight required for your chosen species.

DON'T BE A CHUMP WARNING

Old-school thinking was to dig a huge hole and fill it with soil and compost, but new-school thinking is to dig a hole deep and wide enough for the roots, widening toward the top and using the same soil you dug out of the ground. This way the tree will spread out into the area instead of just clinging to its cushy composted hole, and then could become top-heavy and prone to falling over in high winds. Hopefully you've added a layer of compost to that entire area already, instead of just down in the hole. If not, go back to the soil chapter. Chump!

2. Dig a substantial hole, at least twice as wide as the root ball's diameter, so the roots can spread. Dig down to the same depth that the tree was at in the container or twice as deep as the root ball if the tree came bare root or in a ball of burlap. Leave a small cone of undisturbed soil in the center of the hole.

3. Place the roots in the hole, over the cone, and use the soil you took out to fill back in around the tree's roots. Fill with water when you're halfway done and wait for the water to absorb. Then add in the rest of the soil and water again.

4. Shovel in any remaining soil and pack it down firmly. Tie a stake to the tree trunk if wind is expected and the tree is a bit scrawny. You can remove the stake after the first year.

5. Add a 2-inch layer of mulch to the top of the soil to moderate the soil temperature. Keep the mulch 1 foot away from the tree trunk to encourage good air circulation and avoid disease or rodent problems.

6. Water the tree every day for the first week. Then wean off to every 3 days. A month later, water the tree deeply, preferably with a slow-dripping garden hose, and continue to do this every week or two during the first year, depending on the temperature and when rain isn't present. Continue to monitor the tree during this critical time.

7. Pat yourself on the back for taking this most forward-thinking environmental step!

In the first year, fertilize your new tree three times—spring, summer, and fall—with a couple shovelfuls of compost or a balanced organic fertilizer at the canopy's drip line. After that, you can fertilize once a year in the spring.

Watering Trees

You can begin watering established trees in the spring when you see buds begin to swell or when leaves appear. Watering trees is different from watering smaller landscape plants. Frequently sprinkling the top inch of soil around a tree is not only a waste of water but it's unhealthy for the tree. Trees appreciate infrequent, slow, and very deep watering. The first year you may water trees often, especially during the dry summer months, but after that, trees can be watered twice a month in the summer, preferably with a garden hose or a soaker hose instead of a drip system. You'll want to place the hose at the circular drip line (the outer edge of the tree's canopy). Your mission is to get 5 to 10 gallons of water down for every inch of trunk diameter. A nice slow soaking will reach down deeply and help keep the tree healthy

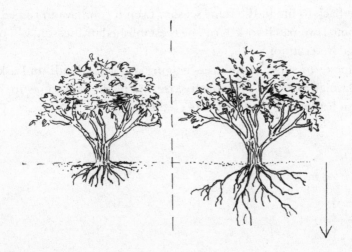

Lay out a garden hose or a soaker hose around the drip line of the tree and water slowly, aiming to reach down to 2 feet.

enough to avoid disease and pests. Most of a tree's water-absorbing roots are in the top 2 feet of the soil, so make sure to water 2 to 3 feet deep. You can purchase a soil probe to see how far down you're watering or try an 18-inch flat-head screwdriver.

In California's hot, drought-prone summer, I like to take a garden hose and lay it on the ground at the edge of the tree's leaves. I set an alarm for 20 to 30 minutes and let the water slowly drip into the ground. You can move the hose to a few positions around the tree, if you have time. Make sure to turn off the hose the minute the alarm goes off or you'll forget.

Last, as I mentioned in Chapter 6, when there is a drought in your area, water trees first! If there are water restrictions in your area, always water the trees first and forget about your perfect petunias and your lazy lawn. It can take 20 years for a young tree to reach the size of an existing 20-year-old tree. Who has that kind of patience? Most lawns can go unwatered for the summer and turn brown but still come back to life in the rainy season. Even if you have to reseed or do some lawn patchwork, it can be reestablished in a season, whereas a large tree cannot.

I spoke to some of my tree-hugging arborist friends and asked them which were some trouble-free trees to plant. They came up with a great list (which I will now take credit for).

Eleven Popular Ornamental Trees

Tree	Zones	Description	Cultivation
Camellia (*Camellia japonica*)	5–9	Dark green, shiny leaves; large pink flowers in early spring	Height: 6 to 12 feet; partial shade; rich, slightly acidic soil
Ornamental crab apple (*Malus*)	3–9	Many gorgeous varieties; pink and white flower clusters in the early spring; many set small fruits; common varieties: 'Beverly', 'Butterball', 'Pink Perfection'	Height: 15 to 40 feet; prefer cool, moist climate and sun; well-drained, loamy soil
Japanese black pine (*Pinus thunbergii*)	1–9	Broad, conical shape with sharp-pointed green needles	Height: 70 feet, but can be kept smaller; any soil; salt and drought tolerant
Japanese flowering cherry (*Prunus serrulata*)	5–8	Pink bell-shaped flower clusters in spring	Height: 20 feet; fertile, well-drained soil
Japanese maple (*Acer palmatum*)	1–9	Red early-spring foliage turns green and then scarlet orange in fall	Height: 15 feet; any normal soil
Jeffrey pine (*Pinus jeffreyi*)	1–9	Bluish green long needles in clusters of three; straight trunk	Height: 60 feet; any normal soil; native to West Coast
Pink-flowering dogwood (*Cornus florida* 'Rubra')	1–9	Large pink flowers in spring	Height: 20 feet, but can be kept smaller; partial shade; normal soil; native to eastern United States
White-flowering dogwood (*Cornus florida* 'Cherokee Princess')	1–9	Abundant small white flower clusters in spring	Height: 20 feet, but can be kept smaller; partial shade; normal soil; native to eastern United States

Tree	Zones	Description	Cultivation
Giant sequoia (*Sequoiadendron giganteum*)	1–10	Conical shape with spiky needles and a pine scent; probably the world's largest living thing	Height: 300 feet, but it's a slow grower; full sun or partial shade; well-drained soil; needs water when young but then survives stupendously with very little care; plant only where room for its wide trunk; native to California but hardy enough to grow in virtually any climate
Saucer magnolia (*Magnolia × soulangiana*)	1–9	Stunning pink saucer-shaped flowers in early spring	Height: 25 feet, but can be kept smaller; moist, fertile soil
Star magnolia (*Magnolia stellata*)	1–9	Profuse starlike white flowers in early spring; slow grower with yellow foliage in the fall	Height: 10 feet, but can be kept smaller; well-drained fertile soil; hardy

A PLANT RECOMMENDATION FROM THE
DIRT DIVA ROYAL HORTICULTURAL SOCIETY

Alcea rosea
COMMON NAME: hollyhock

Hollyhocks are every cottage gardener's dream flower. Most grow up to 6 feet tall with slightly peony- or saucer-shaped large flowers in a range of colors, including pink, purple, white, yellow, and even chocolate! These charming, old-fashioned plants will invite butterflies and hummingbirds to visit. Cut back after each stalk blooms and you may get a second bloom. Plant in the back of the border and make sure it has good air circulation, as they are prone to rust. Good winter cleanup of debris can help minimize the spores.

ORIGIN: Asia
HARDINESS: Zones 4–10
GROWING REQUIREMENTS: Hollyhocks are moderately frost hardy but must be sheltered from wind. Plant in sun in a rich, heavy well-drained soil. Water moderately. Deer resistant. Self-seeds.

THE UNIVERSAL BOTANICAL
WHAAA–WHAA RATING: **5**

12

Ground Covers

WHO YA GONNA CALL?

A ground cover is a group of moderately low-growing plants that you use to blanket an area where you don't want to grow a lawn or a weed patch. Ground covers are not maintenance free, but they're less needy, most can thrive on far less water than a lawn requires, and most are willing to multitask! They look pretty, they prevent erosion by holding soil in place, and they compete with weeds. Many spread and flower easily. They can also be planted underneath trees where there's too much shade and competition from tree roots for grass or other plants. Most ground covers spread from underground runners or they can set a root wherever a node touches the ground. Just like that! They're a fantastic long-term solution for an area or a border you don't have time to take care of and can't afford to pave over, but just want the weeds to stop growing. They're also a fantastic idea if you're growing weary of your lawn.

WHY I'M NOT A FAN OF THE LAWN

Here are a few blades of glory for you from Debbie Downer: The U.S. Fish and Wildlife Service reports that homeowners use up to 10 times more chemical pesticides per acre than farmers use on crops. Lawn-care pesticides are not tested for their chronic health effects, unless they are licensed for food uses.

"Children can be exposed to lawn-care pesticides by playing near an area where pesticides are being applied or by playing outside following a pesticide application, drinking or bathing in water contaminated with lawn-care pesticides, or from parental exposure to lawn-care chemicals during the child's gestation or prior to conception," writes Yale University professor John Wargo, one of the nation's leading experts in pesticide policy, in "Risks from Lawn-Care Pesticides" (Environment & Human Health Inc., 2003).

A 2007 Swedish environmental report in the *Journal of the American Chemical Society* notes that spending an hour mowing your lawn can spew nearly the same amount of oily pollution into the air as a 100-mile car trip. Running a leaf blower for half an hour generates as much pollution as driving a car 110 miles, claim Sierra Club researchers, and all together, gas-powered lawn-care equipment contributes 10 to 12 percent of the nation's air pollution, claims the Environmental Protection Agency.

On top of the careless, senseless, and wasteful overuse of fertilizers and pesticides, homeowners are also using 40 to 60 percent of their summer water allotment on their lawn. *Is a section of tedious turf really worth all the lethal fanfare?!*

Choosing Ground Covers

If I've just caused you or your lawn to break down in tears, it's time to end that codependent relationship and consider chipping away at sections of your lawn slowly and replacing them with ground covers.

When choosing ground covers, think about mixing shape, texture, and color. Lilies, ferns, herbs, wildflowers, vines, and ornamental grasses can be fine options. Ferns go well with hostas and wild ginger in a shady area. *Ajuga*, also called bugle weed, is a fast grower with absolutely no maintenance, yet it flowers happily off in light shade. Try mixing a few different varieties together. Another runner-up is lady's mantle (*Alchemilla mollis*). This plant is ready to serve and step on any weed in her path. It has a long summer flowering season with tiny chartreuse flowers, and the foliage is pretty as well. It'll grow in sun or part shade and is not picky about soil. It can even adapt well to drought conditions and will self-sow.

For a small space with little foot traffic, try planting the airy-fairy foamflower (*Tiarella cordifolia*) or chamomile (*Chamaemelum nobile*). Both are slow growers. A pretty ground cover, which is also a nutritious cover crop, is crown vetch (*Coronilla varia*). This herbaceous perennial grows about 2 feet high and produces pink pea-like girly flowers in the summer (Zones 6–8). It does best in full sun and can stand poor soil and drought. The cultivar 'Penngift' is one of the toughest. Another wonderfully drought-tolerant choice is lamb's ear (*Stachys byzantina*). The light gray, felty foliage sits under erect spikes of small lavender flowers in the summer. This is a hardy and lovely plant that has a reputation of being invasive, but I say, bring it on! I use it as a border plant in my front yard. If you like just the fuzzy leaves and not the flower stalks, try 'Silver Carpet' (Zones 5–10).

Planting Ground Covers

At the nursery, look for the ground-cover section and find the flats (shallow boxes of one type of plant). This is the most economical way to go. Each flat is packed with 12 to 24 seedlings ready to plant. If you have a large area, you can buy more than one flat and mix and match two to three different ground covers that are right for your chosen area.

If this is a brand-new area and you haven't top-dressed it with compost twice a year, as suggested in Chapter 4, then you'll need to do some amending here. Loosen the soil in the area where you'll be planting down about 6 inches and amend the soil with compost. Break up any clods. Water the soil, and you're ready to plant.

If you're using a fabric weed block to help suppress weeds, place it over the soil next. It's up to you if you want to add a fabric barrier. I usually don't when planting ground covers, but every once in a while I do. It all depends how much of a life you have. If the area you're planting in is really susceptible to weeds and you don't want to be out there pulling any weeds at all, go ahead and use the fabric. Just know that the plants will have less room to grow and spread, but they will do just fine. You'll cut an X in the fabric and fold back the points to expose the soil wherever you're placing a plant. Use a hand trowel to dig a hole. Gently loosen the fragile plant from the flat and place it in the hole.

SPACING

Space most 1-gallon plants 18 to 24 inches apart; 4-inch plants, 12 to 18 inches apart; and plants like periwinkle or ivy in flats, 10 to 12 inches apart. Water well and then cover with a 2-inch layer of mulch such as bark chips. Ground covers need regular water until they're established a few seasons down the road, so don't forget to water. If you have a drip system, make sure to add drip emitters to this newly planted section. If you need a path to get to them to water, add a few stepping-stones.

EXTRA CREDIT

Read environmental historian Ted Steinberg's *American Green: The Obsessive Quest for the Perfect Lawn* (W.W. Norton & Co., 2007) to learn about the detrimental lawn lunacy that has severely polluted our land and water since the early 1950s.

If you still have some turf left, learn how to maintain it in a safe and sustainable way. Pick up a copy of Paul Tukey's *Organic Lawn Care Manual* (Storey Publishing, 2007). This book is my lawn bible.

Some Common Ground Covers for Sun

Plant	Description
Artemisia	Silver gray leaves
Common violet (*Viola*)	Sun or shade; hardy; fast growing with sweet purple flowers
Cinquefoil (*Potentilla*)	Forms a green mat with yellow flowers
Evening primrose (*Oenothera*)	Very drought tolerant; white or yellow flowers
Heather	Nice leaf textures with cute flowers; many varieties
Lilyturf (*Liriope spicata*)	Dark green grass with summer blue flower stalks; easy!
Rock cress (*Arabis*)	Evergreen foliage; spring flowers
Rockrose (*Cistus*)	Papery rose-type flowers; drought tolerant
Snow-in-summer (*Cerastium tomentosum*)	Gorgeous, generous white flowers in spring and summer but hides the rest of the year
St. John's wort (*Hypericum*)	Buttercup yellow flowers; red berries
Stonecrop (*Sedum*)	Luv it; drought tolerant and so easy and happy to serve
Thyme (*Thymus*)	Sensationally scented; tiny purple flowers; makes a nice green carpet
Yarrow (*Achillea*)	Drought tolerant; flowers invite many beneficial insects

Some Common Ground Covers for Shade

Plant	Description
Bear's-breeches (*Acanthus*)	A tall, stalk-like plant similar to foxglove but not as endearing; blooms all summer with little care
Carpet bugle (*Ajuga*)	Luv it; fast grower; can handle part-sun; bold blue spring flowers
English ivy (*Hedera helix*)	There are many noninvasive varieties available; great on slopes
Hosta (*Hosta*)	Notable foliage
Lady's mantle (*Alchemilla*)	Scalloped leaves, lime green with lacy spring flowers
Lily-of-the-valley (*Convallaria majalis*)	Fragrant white bell-shaped flowers; fast grower; dies back in winter
Periwinkle (*Vinca*)	Evergreen, white, pink, or blue flowers
Star jasmine (*Trachelospermum*)	Part-sun, light shade; good as tall vine or ground cover
Sweet woodruff (*Galium odoratum*)	Tiny white flowers with woodsy, fragrant leaves
Wild ginger (*Asarum canadense*)	Spreads rapidly into a bell-shaped green mat
Rat-stripper (*Paxistima canbyi*)	No idea about this one; just liked the name

Myosotis
COMMON NAME: forget-me-not

Forget-me-not spreads prolifically each year and
is a welcome source of early-spring bloom,
proudly displaying its dense clusters of tiny
blue flowers with yellow eyes. This annual reseeds
generously and looks fabulous in clumps among
spring bulbs. The cultivar 'Blue Ball' is good for
edging. How can you turn down a name like
that?

ORIGIN: Europe and Asia
HARDINESS: Zones 5–10
GROWING REQUIREMENTS: Plants thrive best in rich soil
and in light, cool shade where they are protected from
hot sun. Does not require fertilizing and needs little
watering. This carefree plant is seldom bothered
by diseases or pests and is deer resistant. Plant one
charming six-pack, and it will reseed for years to come. Go
get one!

THE UNIVERSAL BOTANICAL
WHAAA–WHAA RATING: **1**

13

Shall Hell Be Paved with Weeds?

Here's a little morsel to make you even more miserable about weeds: A purslane weed can drop 52,000 seeds from *one* plant. There's an old saying, "One year of seeds, seven years of weeds." Well, it's even worse. Only 10 to 20 percent of those seeds will sprout each year and about 50 percent will remain viable after 7 years. In 20 years there will still be 1 percent of the original seeds. That's not counting any new purslane plants setting seeds. Makes you want to hang up the towel on gardening and go back to crocheting or name-dropping instead, doesn't it?

Though we all cringe when we see weeds shooting up in our soil, it's best to face the fact that you'll be doing some serious hand weeding a few times a year. Getting rid of all weeds is impossible. A more realistic goal for weeding is to minimize the time you're outside hand weeding. You'll need to do a good deal of manual labor in early spring after the winter rains, before the numerous amount of spring-time weeds set seed. After that, periodically throughout the year, you'll have smaller weed-pulling/neck-hurting projects.

"Do weeds have any redeeming qualities?" one might ask. Fo' shizzle! Many are a nectar source for honeybees and some butterflies, a habitat for beneficial predators and parasites, cover and food for birds and other vertebrates, a potential source of therapeutic pharmaceuticals; many are useful in reduction of dust and erosion; and all are helpful in aerating compacted soil. Common weeds such as black medic, white clover, and Japanese clover all fix nitrogen from the atmosphere. The ubiquitous dandelion is edible, brings calcium and other nutrients to the surface, leaves behind canals for the earthworm's travel, and is an early nectar source for bees. That said, too many weeds can spread disease or pest infestations and compete with our beloved plants, leaving us continuously on a search-and-destroy mission.

The Devil Weeds

There are two main weeds: annual weeds and perennial weeds. Annuals complete their life cycle in a year, while perennial weeds will stalk you, surviving for 3 or more years. An annual weed only grows for one season, creating thousands of seeds that get blown all over the garden. A perennial weed is spread by underground stems, root parts, seeds, tubers, corms, and cheap gossip. Perennial weeds' roots have to be dug up to stop their ghastly invasion. I rarely want to use the word *hate*, and botanists nonchalantly like to say that "a weed is simply a plant out of place," but perennial weeds some days will drive me down the highway to hate. Every March, I find myself *hating*, so a few years ago I bought a scuffle hoe. Every gardener should have a scuffle hoe. It has a horizontal blade for cutting weeds just below the surface. It's great exercise and it's fun and you can take out all of your aggression on "the man" or your boss or at me, because I said it was *fun*, when it's actually slightly exhausting and your neck may ache after. Go see your chiropractor and then pay your preteen child and his friends to stop being vidiots and get outdoors to help weed.

ANNUAL WEEDS

The best time to attack annual weeds is shortly after it rains or watering them. Rain will germinate hundreds of weed seeds. But don't touch the soil when plants or soil are still wet. Let it all dry out, or you'll spread disease, compact the soil, and blame me.

Once the soil is dry, rake or scuffle hoe the newly formed weed sprouts. This will wipe out most weed seeds before they come up to the surface. In the spring, well after the winter rains, you may have to rake the top layer of soil three to four more times till you can be safe from weed seeds. Stay strong, soldier! Because these new weed seedlings have not produced seeds, you can toss these weed sprouts into your compost pile. After years of amending your soil with compost

---

THE TROUBLEMAKERS

SOME COMMON ANNUAL WEEDS
Barnyard grass, black medic, Carolina geranium, carpetweed, chickweed, crab grass, goosegrass, Japanese clover, lamb's quarters, mallow, knotweed, and witch grass

SOME COMMON PERENNIAL WEEDS
Bermuda grass, bindweed, chicory, curly dock, dandelion, English daisy, nut grass, plantain, purslane, quack grass, Queen Anne's lace, violet, white clover, yellow wood sorrel

Take a sample to your local nursery or local Master Gardener office to see which weed has moved onto your lot without an invitation.

---

and not using synthetic fertilizers, your soil will be loose, so you won't have to work so hard to get weeds out. They'll pull right up.

PERENNIAL WEEDS

Some of the most common evildoers of the perennial weeds are quack grass, Bermuda grass, nut grass, and bindweed (which can penetrate 16 feet deep!). These all have widespread root systems.

If you don't attack these weeds in the spring, you'll be a dollar short and a day late, and the weeds will drop their thousands of weed seeds to exasperate you for years to come. But the key in pulling perennial weeds is going the distance. That means, *digging them completely out,* making sure not to leave a remaining runner or tuber underground. One of the best times to dig these intruders out is right after they bloom but before they form seed heads. This is when they're loafing around telling knock-knock jokes, storing the least amount of energy underground, and you can sneak up on them and attack.

Flamers Are Hot!

And now, for the Pyro-Diva . . . There's nothing like a little fire to get you to feel like you're winning the weed battle. Flamers are portable gas torches that will burn up the water in a plant's cells in a second. They're a good alternative to using herbicides and work especially well on young annual or perennial weeds or weeds in a row of crops or pernicious weeds growing in between pavers. Fire it up! A flamer is costlier than a scuffle hoe, but it's sure a lot more fun. Prices average $100. (And it can also be used as a snow-melter or de-icer in winter. You will be the envy of your neighbors . . . or any 12-year-old boy.) If you're going to get one, read the directions and use all safety precautions. Wear heavy boots and stomp out any flare-ups, and have a hose within easy reach. It's all fun and games till someone burns down the neighbor's boat parked on the dead lawn across the street.

PRESPROUTING AND SOIL SOLARIZATION

Another weed-destroying technique is presprouting. Presprouting is helpful if you have raised beds or a patch of land where you grow vegetables in the spring each year. A month before you plant your vegetables, amend your soil with compost and water this area as if you're planting your spring garden. In a week or two, you'll see many weed seedlings, mostly annuals. Gently scrape off the seedlings. Water again and wait two more weeks. Scrape again gently. You can now plant your garden. Presprouting isn't an exact science, so don't hold me accountable if you still have weeds. You'll have some weeds but many fewer than before.

Soil solarization is another option for a small area, a vegetable garden or a raised bed. You won't be able to grow anything there for about 2 months. In July, remove all weeds and plants from the raised bed. Till or rake the soil free of clumps, prepare the soil for planting, and level the soil. Water the soil. Purchase a clear tarp. (Transparent plastic will allow more heat to penetrate than colored tarps will. Polyethylene plastic one or two mil thick works best.) Roll the plastic out over the soil. Smooth out air pockets and pin it down. Wait 5 to 6 weeks in full sun for maximum treatment and remove plastic. This is effective for killing plant pathogens as well as weeds in the top foot of soil, so you get two for the price of one! Amend the soil with fresh compost, since some of the good bacteria and fungi are now fried. This would be a good time to plant a nitrogen-fixing cover crop for a few months, before planting a vegetable or flower garden on this soil.

LESS TOXIC HERBICIDES

I don't use chemical herbicides because several inorganic herbicides have been found to persist in the soil for many years. Several have already polluted groundwater by runoff into our sewers and streams, and many are toxic to humans and animals. As a result, the EPA has restricted many inorganic weed-killers from home gardens. Unfortunately, many are still available and have ingredients in them that have been shown to disrupt the human endocrine system, causing changes in estrogen and testosterone levels, thyroid problems, reproductive abnormalities, and prostate cancer.

Some newer less toxic products contain clove oil, which is said to work well on young broadleaf weeds. There are also products made with acetic acid (strong vinegar) and sometimes blended with citric acid that do an adequate job on young grasses. Some products contain both clove oil and acetic acid and work well on a broad group of weeds. Two citrus-based, biodegradable herbicides that I've heard have worked successfully on various weeds are Nature's Avenger Organic Herbicide and BurnOut. A homemade option is to mix two-thirds apple cider vinegar with one-third dish soap in a spray bottle. The dish soap will help the vinegar stick to the weeds. The roots will still be strong and slightly infuriated, so you'll have to redo this a couple of times till you eventually wear out the root system. Never spray on windy days, and always wear gloves and goggles.

Corn gluten is a safe, natural herbicide that works well to keep crab grass and some other weed seeds from ever germinating. The powder can be spread on lawns or in perennial beds where you're not planting seeds. The critical part of using corn gluten is timing. It must be spread when crab grass is about to germinate. This is the same time as when your azaleas, dogwoods, and forsythias begin to bloom. Depending on where you live, this is usually late winter or early spring.

Where to find these safer products is yet another task for home-

DIRT DIVA TIP

Weed for 20 minutes and then go take a break and hit it hard the next day, or later that afternoon, or after a frappuccino. Take it slow. Let the springtime weed project take a few weekends to complete, and always put on your iPod so your neighbors won't stop to chitchat with you and slow you down. You're on a mission.

Recommended 20-Minute iPod Set

"Midnight Train to Georgia," by Gladys Knight and the Pips

"The Saints Are Coming," by U2 and Green Day

"Stupid Girls," by Pink

"Son of a Preacher Man," by Dusty Springfield

"Gone, Gone, Gone," by Robert Plant and Alison Krauss

owners. They're usually hidden in the far back of the garden center if they even carry them at all. Ask the store manager why all the weed-killers/lawn chemicals that have links to "serious adverse chronic effects in humans" are always sitting on the shelves right at the cash register. Then go shop at your local plant nursery where safer options are available.

Last, mulch must always be a part of your weed-control scheme. Mulch will smother the overambitious weeds, making it difficult for them to penetrate as it blocks light from reaching the soil. Take those weeds to the dark side! The best way to deter weeds in your garden is to avoid bare ground. Always covering exposed soil with mulch or ground cover or both will help significantly.

EXTRA CREDIT

Weedless Gardening, by Lee Reich (Workman, 2001)

A PLANT RECOMMENDATION FROM THE
DIRT DIVA ROYAL HORTICULTURAL SOCIETY

Papaver somniferum 'Drama Queen'
COMMON NAME: poppy

This variety of poppy is a crimson showy girl with shades of indigo. She's easy-peasy. Just some amended soil, average water, and full sun or light shade is required. Poppies grow well in rock gardens, flowerbeds, and containers. Most will reseed if you let them go to seed. 'Drama Queen' will grow 2 to 3 feet tall and bloom in the spring.

ORIGIN: Middle East
HARDINESS: Zones 7–10
GROWING REQUIREMENTS: Fully frost hardy, they prefer sun over shade and deep, moist well-drained soil. Low to average water.

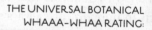

THE UNIVERSAL BOTANICAL
WHAAA–WHAA RATING: **3**

PART THREE

Flower Power

Starting off this section is Chapter 14, "Seed Catalog Junkies: United We Shop and Sow." We've lost many heirloom (traditional) varieties of flower and food seed in the last century, leaving us with shrinking options at the supermarket and plant nursery. By choosing heirloom seeds, we're growing history and promoting genetic diversity. A tutorial on sowing your own seeds indoors proceeds with helpful tips.

Next is Chapter 15, "Plant Bulbs Now: Impress Your Friends Later." Bulbs are usually the first flowers we see in the early spring, reminding us that winter is almost over and the growing season is gearing up. We backyard geeks live for this moment! Learn about the many summer- and fall-flowering bulbs to add to your garden as well.

Chapter 16, "Roses Are My Weakness," is just what it says. My mom was obsessed with roses too. She'd grown roses as a child in Israel, supposedly. But a few weeks before she died, she told me she'd been too poor to grow roses and had planted only radish seeds in her ghetto garden. I haven't interrogated the relatives on this because, well, radishes? Bah!

In Chapter 17, "Cut Flowers That'll Make Your Friends Weep," and Chapter 18, "Butterflies in the 'Hood," you'll learn about growing flowers for long-lasting floral bouquets and attracting butterflies to your yard. Many of the flowers that flourish in an indoor vase are the same flowers that also attract various pollinators. You'll be multitasking: doing a good deed for your neighborhood and making your friends think you're as resourceful as Martha Stewart, at the same time.

Chapter 19, "Pruning, Dividing, Cutting, and Running," will be handy to refer back to time and time again. Most flowering perennials and shrubs require annual pruning as well as periodic dividing to stay healthy. It's impossible to remember when to prune or divide every plant in your yard, but I've listed some of the most common ones. You'll also learn how to make cuttings out of your favorite roses or perennials so you'll have more of them for your yard or to give away to friends. This will keep your friends and relatives in your back pocket, where they belong.

14

Seed Catalog Junkies

UNITED WE SHOP AND SOW

A few years ago I traded in my black boot obsession for an equally disturbing fixation on organic heirloom seeds. These are seeds of plants with history to them. Many of them were grown in the eighteenth to early twentieth century. Lucky for us, many farmers, botanists, and home gardeners saved these flower and food seeds to pass on to future generations.

There are many outstanding seed companies to choose from. I support those that grow seeds organically and have biological diversity. Diversity is nature's survival tool. Here's a little seedy data for you: In 1900, Americans grew 7,000 named varieties of apples. About 10 percent of those exist today. In the last century 30,000 vegetable varieties have become extinct. Between 1908 and 1983, 92.8 percent of lettuce varieties were lost.

I know what you're thinking. Who needs all those apples? And, who wants all that lettuce? Just give us some crunchy iceberg, what do we know? According to the Seed Savers Exchange (www.seedsavers.org), whose mission is to "save the world's diverse but endangered garden heritage for future generations," biological diversity is being lost at an alarming rate. Here on our amazing planet Earth we require diversity in our rain forests, grasslands, deserts, ecosystems, and creatures. This diversity is also critical in our food crops. When we plant a wide variety of flowers, herbs, vegetables, and fruit, we not only provide habitat for beneficial insects and important pollinators but provide a more varied and nutritious diet for humans. *Is it all about us, after all? C'mon, that's so elementary!*

For example, in 1970, a corn blight devastated more than 15 percent of the North American corn crop. The corn was particularly susceptible to the blight because over 70 percent of the corn being grown in the United States came from the same parent lines. Maintaining heirlooms prevents occurrences like the corn blight. Let's take the potato famine in 1840s Ireland. Farmers there subsisted on only one staple crop—a single variety of potato. When disease wiped it out, about a million people died of famine-related causes.

Hard fact: A diva cannot survive on potatoes alone.

Never fear. Our saviors are here! Here are a few seed companies I have a fondness for. All of them sell either organic or heirloom flower and/or food seeds and share a strong commitment to sustainable agriculture and a future full of crop diversity:

Johnny's Selected Seeds, Winslow, Maine (www.johnnyseeds.com)
D. Landreth Seed Company, Baltimore, Maryland (www.landreth seeds.com)
Larner Seeds, Bolinas, California (www.larnerseeds.com)
Native Seeds Tucson, Arizona (www.nativeseeds.org)
Seeds of Change, El Guique, New Mexico (www.seedsofchange.com)
Stokes Seeds, Buffalo, New York (www.stokesseeds.com)
Baker Creek Heirloom Seeds, Petaluma, California (www.rare seeds.com)

Renee's Garden, Felton, California (www.reneesgarden.com)

Territorial Seed Company, London Springs, Oregon (www.territo
rialseed.com)

The Cook's Garden, Warminster, Pennsylvania (www.cooksgarden
.com)

Let's Sow Some Seeds!

Every February I grow seeds indoors, and at the time when they're about to be moved outdoors to harden off or, as I call it, "go to middle school," I get a call to travel on assignment and the poor seeds die of neglect. Seeds are tender and needy, so if you're going to grow them, be prepared to be a doting mother for at least a month! It's well worth it when and *if* the seeds turn into seedlings and survive all the way to you transplanting them in your garden. You'll feel a great sense of accomplishment. Sowing seeds can be done anywhere. If you're an apartment dweller or live out in the country, it's a fun project to try. If you live in the city and don't have a garden, you can grow seeds to give seedlings to friends who will happily grow them for you in their yard. Though farmers grow seeds in greenhouses all year long, many home gardeners will sow seeds in the late winter to plant in the ground in spring. Ten fast-growing perennials that flower their first year from seed are yarrow, butterfly weed, Shasta daisy, black-eyed Susan, blanketflower, gaura, delphinium, rose campion, aster, and speedwell.

STEPS TO SUCCESSFUL SEED STARTING
Scarification or Soaking
Many seeds with hard outer shells will have a better chance of sprouting if you nick them around a bit with a knife, file, or sandpaper. You don't want to go too crazy on the seed, so I suggest gently rubbing against a piece of sandpaper or a nail file for beginners.

You could soak hard seeds instead of nicking them. Put seeds in a bowl with warm water and let them soak overnight. This is especially good for peas, corn, and beans. Don't leave them any longer than overnight or they'll become waterlogged.

Containers

There are many fine containers to choose from. You could use the old six-pack plastic container from the nursery or even paper cups. Just make sure you wash them out with a tiny bit of bleach in water to sterilize them before planting in them.

I've found that peat containers work best for impatient and second-rate seed starters like myself. I need all the help I can get. So I always buy a flat made of peat moss with 24 or so separate compartments that you can later just tear off each section and plant the biodegradable little box straight into your soil. This greatly reduces transplant shock. (Jiffy Peat Pots and CowPots are both good options and are available at most nurseries.)

Pinchushion flower (*Scabiosa*) is easily grown from seed.

You'll want to moisten the peat pots before you add the growing medium (potting mix), so run the pots under some cool water first so they can absorb some moisture.

Garden soil is too dense to plant seeds in. Instead, purchase a bag of seed-starting mix or potting mix. The teeny-tiny roots of your seedlings can't penetrate garden soil and they'll go bust on you; then you'll blame me. A soil-less seed-starting mix such as a mix of vermiculite, cocopeat (which is a renewable resource, unlike peat moss), and perlite will protect your seeds from damping off and dying on you. All of these increase aeration and drainage. You'll find this mix at most nurseries and garden centers. You'll want to mix this growing medium in a bowl with water to dampen it. Let it sit in a strainer for some time to drain and then use it to fill your peat pots. (If the medium is too dry, germination won't occur, and if it's too wet, the seeds could rot. Isn't seed sowing fun!?) Fill each pot with the mixture.

Sowing

Once your growing container is filled, poke a few tiny holes into the potting mix with a pencil and place three seeds in each section or pot. The seeds should be buried to a depth four times their own diameter. Larger seeds will be planted farther down, and fine seeds will be closer to the top. I always plant three seeds so I have a good success rate. Cover the pots with a thin layer of plastic wrap on top to seal in moisture and speed up germination. Some planting trays come with a plastic cover. You could even place the tray in a large, clear plastic bag, lightly tied closed at the end. Place your tray in a dark, warm area of your home, and check on it each day or two to see if there are sprouts.

Watering and Light

These are the two critical parts of seed starting. This is what makes you a winner or a loser. Newly planted seeds should be watered liberally and gently with a light spray or mist. You should have to water them only once or twice before you see the seeds germinate or sprout. I like to add a heating mat under the tray to keep the seeds all toasty.

Once germinated (when you see some little sprouts popping up), all seedlings need to be in the spotlight. This will make them strong and healthy plants. A south-facing window will work, but remember to rotate the container daily. You could invest in a fluorescent light, which I highly recommend if you're going to grow seeds each year. Seedlings need 12 to 16 hours of light each day. If the light isn't strong enough or is too far from the tray, the seedlings will grow tall and spindly. Once germinated, remove the plastic cover if you had one on, and water often. Gently water in between the seedling rows. Soon the *cotyledon* will come up. This is the first tiny leaf or set of leaves, which are food storage cells. Soon after, you'll see the first true leaf or leaves sprout. Once you see them, it's time to celebrate. Bring on a nice bottle of liquid organic fertilizer or fish emulsion, dilute it with water, and let those new leaves party like rock stars weekly!

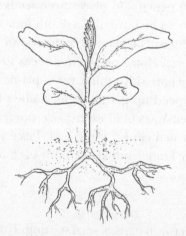

The second leaf or set of leaves are the true leaves.

Hardening Off and Transplanting

Once the seedlings have developed four true leaves, it's time to thin them. You want to leave about 1 inch between each seedling. Gently cut out the weaker-looking and overcrowded seedlings with a pair of scissors, at the soil line. Once frost in your area waves its chilly good-bye, you can begin placing your pampered seed tray outside for a few hours a day, in light shade. You'll want to introduce them to the outdoors (or real world) incrementally. Bring in the tray at night. After 3 days, leave them in the sun for a good part of the day. Gradually lengthen their outdoor visit.

Once this week of hardening off is done and you've worked your soil with organic matter, you can carefully plant your peat boxes, peat pellets, or very tender seedlings directly into the ground or into a pot. Gently water every day for a week and keep a close eye on your seedlings, watching for slugs, cold temperatures, or dehydration. I'd

Seed Savers Exchange (www.seedsavers.org) is a nonprofit organization of gardeners who save and share heirloom seeds. Founded in 1975 by Diane and Kent Whealy, Seed Savers Exchange has a scenic 890-acre headquarters located near Decorah, Iowa. As a member of Seed Savers Exchange, you'll have access to over 11,000 unique varieties of heirloom vegetables, fruits, grains, flowers, and herbs through the Seed Savers annual yearbook. Thousands of heirlooms are grown in certified organic fields. What I like about this organization is that we can still enjoy the same flowers our grandparents once grew, such as *Alcea rosea* or the "outhouse hollyhock," famous on Iowa farmsteads for over a century. Refined ladies searched for the hollyhocks and didn't have to ask where the bathroom was! Glad we still have these self-seeding 6- to 9-foot-tall biennials with us. Refined ladies? Not so much.

also pamper them once a week with a light dose of liquid seaweed foliar spray to help them with transplant shock. After 2 weeks out in the big, wide world, you can begin to have a life again. Have faith that, in time, your babies will grow strong, make friends, have iPods glued to their ears, trade away their healthy organic lunch, and text nonstop.

A PLANT RECOMMENDATION FROM THE
DIRT DIVA ROYAL HORTICULTURAL SOCIETY

Cosmos bipinnatus
COMMON NAME: cosmos

Cosmos are cheerful, daisy-like flowers that come in pink, crimson, and white. Many grow over 3 feet tall and bloom for many months in the summer. There's a neighbor down the road who has a trashy front yard, probably knows nothing about gardening, and yet, has 5-foot cosmos blooming and reseeding along her front path all summer long. All of my cosmos seedlings went belly up in the first heat spell. Master Gardeners are supposed to be benevolent, but, well, it's just not fair!

ORIGIN: Mexico
HARDINESS: Zones 2–10; half-hardy annual
GROWING REQUIREMENTS: Average, well-drained soil, heat, and sun and moderate to low water. They attract birds, bees, Monarch butterflies, and many beneficial insects. Cosmos easily self-seed.

THE UNIVERSAL BOTANICAL
WHAAA–WHAA RATING: **3**

15

Plant Bulbs Now

IMPRESS YOUR FRIENDS LATER

Here's the thing about bulbs: Anyone, and I mean anyone, even my sister Sharon with her exotic plastic houseplant collection, can grow a real live flower from a bulb! All you need is a shovel, a bit of phosphorus or compost, and a whole lot of patience. Bulbs and their cousins—the corms, tubers, and rhizomes—are actually all underground storage systems. All will be treated similarly when growing them. Gardeners use the term *bulb* loosely to cover all of these plants. Bulbs are an excellent starter plant for new gardeners. For more experienced gardeners, bulbs are a lovely addition to blend into your garden design. Spring-blooming bulbs can be planted in the ground or in pots in the fall, while summer- and fall-blooming bulbs can be planted in spring to early summer.

Step 1: Shopping

Go to your local nursery or online catalog and drool over blooming bulb photographs. When you're done salivating, choose your few favorite flowers from thousands of spectacular bulbs. That's a valiant challenge! You want to purchase a variety of bulbs that bloom at different times so that you can have garden color for as many months as possible. We all know the tulip eats and breathes for attention and can't live without being center stage in the garden drama. However, there are other bulbs that play supporting roles, which are just as stunning as the tulip and come without all that vanity and baggage. See the following lists for a few of the easiest and prettiest.

THE AWARD-WINNING SUPPORTING CAST
Spring Bloomers to Plant in the Fall

FLOWERING ONION (*ALLIUM*) Happy to be employed in Zones 4–10, alliums thrive in full sun in well-drained soil. Some common cousins in the Allium family are chives, onion, and garlic. Many of these ornamental herbs have gorgeous red-purple globular clusters on top of their tall stalks all summer long with little care.

GRECIAN WINDFLOWER (*ANEMONE BLANDA*) Sweet windflower is a sprightly short anemone flower with blue, pink, or white daisy-like flowers. Zones 6–9. The flowers open in the sun, and many anemones multiply, giving you more flowers each year. Can I get an amen?

SNOWDROP (*GALANTHUS NIVALIS*) Happy in Zones 3–8, snowdrop sometimes pops up in late winter when there is still snow on the ground, making a magical late-winter display. The long-lasting 1-inch flowers are white and sit atop a slender threadlike stalk. Snowdrop thrives in partial shade and increases over the years by seed and by bulb, forming dense clumps.

GRAPE HYACINTH (*MUSCARI*) Grape hyacinth can hold an audience captive with its low-growing blue clustered flowers, which look similar to tiny grapes. Works well in Zones 3–8 and is an easy early bloomer. Most species are 6 to 9 inches tall, but Armenian grape hyacinth is about 1 foot tall. The blue color complements white or yellow daffodils, as they both bloom in very early spring, alerting us that winter is about to close up shop.

CROWN IMPERIAL (*FRITILLARIA IMPERIALIS*) Crown imperial is a remarkable, attention-stealing plant that grows in Zones 4–8. The stems are 2 to 4 feet tall and have 6 to 12 red-orange bell-shaped flowers hanging from them; pretty magnificent. She is a bit higher maintenance than her fellow cast members. Not horribly. I mean, she doesn't ask for room-temperature Evian water, but she does demand full sun, no wind, and to be planted a foot down with compost, or she'll refuse to come out of her trailer.

DAFFODIL (*NARCISSUS*) I love daffodils because they naturalize, meaning they keep multiplying each year without you doing a thing. Before you get too excited though, the bulbs are often eaten by gophers and their underground rodent pals, so you may still have to plant these as an annual. Daffodils are dependable and demand such little care that they are a must! They come in a variety of peachy to white to yellow tones and styles, and can grow in full sun to light shade. They will turn and find the sun no matter where they're planted. Zones 2–9.

ANEMONE BUTTERCUP (*RANUNCULUS*) This is my favorite bulb to plant. They come in so many gorgeous colors and have a cup shape similar to old roses or peonies. Anemone buttercups are easy to grow in sun or light shade and make excellent cut flowers. Zones 7–10.

TULIP (*TULIPA*) Plant our leading ladies before the ground freezes in a sunny to partly shady spot with well-draining soil. These are Mediterranean plants and do best in soil that is slightly on the dry side. It's good to plant them in a flower border between perennials and annuals so that the old foliage will be hidden after the tulip blooms in the spring. Choose different species for a long bloom season. Some early bloomers are single early, double early, Greigii, Kaufmanniana, and Fosteriana. For midseason, try Darwin hybrids and Triumph. For

Fall Bulb-Planting Schedule for Spring Bloomers
Zones 2–3: September
Zones 4–5: Late September to early October
Zones 6–7: Mid-October to early November
Zone 8: November to early December
Zones 9–11: November to mid-December

some late-season choices, try lily-flowered, peony-flowered, single late, parrot, and double late. Zones 2–9.

Summer and Fall Bloomers to Plant in the Spring

BEARDED IRIS *(IRIS)* Bearded iris will tolerate drought and some neglect, so this is a good option for gardeners who live in climates with dry, hot summers. Bold-colored three-petaled flower heads bloom in early summer above tall sword-like leaves. Easy to divide after summer bloom. Zones 3–8.

MONTBRETIA *(CROCOSMIA)* These slender corms from South Africa grow to 3 feet with a branching spike of yellow to orange tubular flowers in early summer. They make good cut flowers and come back every summer without you doing a thing. Zones 6–9.

DAHLIA Dahlias grow from 10 inches, for dwarf types, up to 7 feet tall. Some flower heads are as large as dinner plates with an assortment of colors and textures. They need 6 hours of sun a day to be at their showy best. Here in California, I leave mine in the ground to come back each year, but in Zone 8 or less, you may need to dig them out and store over the winter. Zones 7–10.

GLADIOLAS *(GLADIOLUS)* Gladiolas are a familiar summertime sight in backyards and as cut flowers at farmers markets. Tall, bold-colored spiky flowers often grow 3 to 6 feet tall, and sometimes need staking.

Plant a grouping every 2 weeks to have a summer succession of blooms. Excellent cut flowers. Zones 7–10.

AFRICAN CORN LILY *(IXIA)* These perennial corms are from South Africa and are relatives of the Iris family. They produce absolutely mesmerizing star-shaped flowers in an array of unusual colors on a slender 2-foot stalk. Does best in sun but can stand a bit of shady protection from hot summer sun. Zones 8–10.

LILIES—ASIATIC, HYBRID, TIGER *(LILIUM)* Lilies have a bowl- or trumpet-shaped flower that comes in various colors of pink, red, yellow, orange, maroon, and lilac. There are many, many species to choose from. Most thrive in sun or partial shade in fertile, moist soil. Mulch with compost or shredded bark to keep the soil cool. Feed with compost tea monthly during the summer. Zones 3–8.

Now order away and feel guilty about how much money you just spent on corms and tubers.

Step 2: Planting

Once your bulbs arrive, store them in a dark, dry, and cool area such as a garage. Because bulb roots reach deep down, you'll need to amend your soil just as deep, usually a foot down. Make sure you have good drainage as well. Before planting, mix a few scoops of compost into your soil. To encourage good root and flower growth, I like to add a tablespoon of bonemeal, which is rich in phosphorus, to the bottom of each planting hole.

Many nurseries offer a free bulb-planting chart that lists planting depths for various bulbs. If you can't find one, a good rule of thumb is to dig the hole twice as deep as the diameter of the bulb and lay the bulb on the bottom. An inexpensive tool to use if you have hard clay

WHICH END IS UP?

If not sure, a general rule of thumb is to plant the bulb with the pointy end up and the roots down. If you're still not sure, plant it on its side. The bulb itself, or your backyard trolls, will turn the bulb to the correct direction underground. If still not sure, don't call me. Consult a Ouija board.

soil and lots of bulbs is a bulb planter. This handy scooper will make planting bulbs more enjoyable.

It's best to plant bulbs in clusters of 12 or more. Don't be skimpy. More is good. The larger the bulb, the fewer you need in the cluster or clump. For instance, for large bulbs such as tulips and daffodils, you could use 3 to 5 to a clump, about 1 inch apart in a circle. Set them in the ground firmly, then cover them with soil, water thoroughly, and cover with a 2- to 3-inch layer of mulch or leaves.

Step 3: Maintenance

Another worthy characteristic about bulbs is that they are relatively free of pests and diseases. The only downfall is that rodents may get to them. One option is to dig up a good-size section of your planting area, plant the bulbs, and then lay a piece of chicken wire on top. They'll grow in between the chicken wire. Cover with soil and mulch.

Bulbs look fantastic in pots. I have a few round and rectangular containers in the backyard that weigh a ton, but that doesn't stop me from dragging them out to the front of the house in early spring, when the first daffodils pop up. Remember, you always want to show off your latest garden achievements. Don't leave them hidden in the backyard where no one sees them. That's just plain wrong.

The utterly pathetic thing about bulbs is the fact that you have to keep the old foliage on the bulb for about 6 weeks after it blooms. If you cut off the foliage before it yellows, you sever the bulb's food supply and weaken it for the future. I know. It's a poor design for those of us who like to tidy up nature. But if your soil is in good condition from amending it in the fall, your spring or summer perennials should be coming into their most prolific season and can hide the old bulb's brown foliage.

Step 4: Storing

Many summer-blooming bulbs are not winter hardy and, depending on where you live, they may have to be dug out and stored over the winter months. I live in California, so I don't have to do that. Who has the time? We're busy people. We all can't be out there digging for shriveled up root balls. Whose bright idea was that anyway? If your area endures severe freezes (or you have people), you should dig up the bulbs as soon as they turn black after the first freeze. Wash off the soil and cut off all the foliage. Dry them off in the sun for a few days and then store them in a box filled with sawdust, in a cool, dark place like a garage. If you're like me and don't have time (or people), consider growing bulbs in a large wooden box or pot and move the entire pot to a sunny, protected place in your yard for the winter. If all else fails, buy bulbs as annuals to enjoy for one season only. Oh, listen, I swear I hear the Dutch bulb suppliers clapping, all the way in Holland!

A PLANT RECOMMENDATION FROM THE
DIRT DIVA ROYAL HORTICULTURAL SOCIETY

Lilium superbum
COMMON NAME: Turk's-cap lily

This is one of the largest-flowered and most impressive of the native lilies. Grows easily in damp garden soil and when established, can reach over 7 feet tall with whorls of bell-shaped round unusual blossoms. Native Americans used the bulbs to make soups.

ORIGIN: East Coast of the United States
HARDINESS: Zones 3–10
GROWING REQUIREMENTS: Good drainage is critical. Add in plenty of organic matter. Filtered sun to light shade is okay, but make sure to plant the bulb at least 4 inches deep. Where summers are cool, plant in full sun.

THE UNIVERSAL BOTANICAL
WHAAA–WHAA RATING: **5**

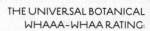

16
Roses Are My Weakness

You may live next door to a rose addict. They're quite common. We seem somewhat normal on the outside but we're not. Especially when spring is in the air. Then we're craving just one more rose bush, promising ourselves it will be the last new rose we plant. Ever. We're done! We're out of room in the yard. Until . . . we realize we can get rid of some other boring shrub and plant another English rose there instead. No one will suspect. We'll divide and conquer at dark wearing a ski mask.

Once you've successfully grown roses, you'll find that roses aren't so hard to grow. They have a reputation of being high maintenance but you just have to understand them. The best way to do this is to do what I've done. *Become a rose.* Start demanding what they do; sun for at least 6 hours a day, drinks, organic food, and lots of attention. Let me know how this goes over with your family and friends . . .

Planting New Rosebushes

Bare-root roses are roses in a dormant state. Late winter is considered the best time to plant bare-root roses but, depending on where you live, you may not be able to plant them until March or April. Check with your local nursery. Never plant a bare-root rose when the ground is frozen or a hard freeze is expected.

You'll pay less for a bare-root rose in winter than for a more established potted rosebush later on in the spring or summer. Order from catalogs or visit your local nursery and do what I do: Stroll around in a rose-possessed stupor, gazing at the color photographs attached to each rose, daydreaming about its 50 soft pink petals; sweet tight buds; majestic cupped blossoms; large mature clusters; the intoxicating damask rose fragrance; and shiny, strong disease-resistant leaves. This mesmerizing state of euphoria is what we in the Dirt Diva Royal Horticultural Society refer to as "rose porn."

Roses grow best in soil that has good drainage, such as sandy loam. Their preferred pH is 6.5. They demand lots of sun and fresh air, so make sure you choose a site with at least 6 hours of direct sun and some discernible air movement. A shady or cramped location will only invite insects and diseases.

My sister Augusta is a rose lover as well as a philosophy professor, so we've had profound existential discussions about life and roses. (Philosophers live for this.) She reads me theories of the more upbeat philosophers, but I keep resorting back to my favorite wet blanket, Jean-Paul Sartre (mostly to annoy her). Sartre wrote, "Hell is other people." To a rose, the queen of the flower, "Hell is other roses." Roses like space and biodiversity, not other roses touching them. Eew! They like to be unique and will be more resistant to pest attacks if they have plenty of air and a diverse group of plants sharing

ROSE LINGO
Types of Roses the Snooties
Like to Talk about with Their Pinkies Up

Hybrid Tea Usually has one large, scented, single flower to a stem, on a plant 3 to 5 feet tall. Blooms repeatedly throughout the summer; has a pompous air about it. Walks like a poodle.

Polyantha Short, compact plant with many smaller flowers growing in clusters. Blooms over a long period; is easy to grow.

Floribunda Cross between a hybrid tea and a polyantha. Hardy and compact with medium-size flowers growing abundantly in clusters.

Grandiflora Can grow to 6 feet tall with large flowers in long-stemmed clusters from summer through fall.

Climbers Have long flexible canes that can be attached to fences, posts, and arbors and can grow 10 to 20 feet long or more. Most are fast climbers, easy to grow, and require minimal pruning.

Miniature Pip-squeaks. Easy to grow, and good in pots on decks. Happy to serve; rarely make a peep.

Shrub More shrub shaped, than urn shaped; usually larger and wilder than other types. Tend to be hardy and disease resistant. A great choice for novice rose growers.

Old Roses (Heritage, Antique) Some of the most common are alba, damask, Bourbon, China, gallica, and Noisette. Old-fashioned looking, taking you back in time. Scented and splendid, but many just bloom once in the spring, sometimes offering a second, less dramatic flush in the summer.

English Roses Have the characteristics of the new roses—repeat blooming and sturdy—with the heavenly old-fashioned fragrance and whimsical charm of old roses. (Available from David Austin Roses at www .davidaustinroses.com.)

their divine world. I like to plant rosemary, lavender, and sages near my roses. They're all sun worshipers, the strong scents of the herbs deter many pests, and best of all, the herbs bloom after the big spring rose bloom so they don't steal the queen of the flower's spotlight.

Going with our "Hell is other roses" hypothesis, it's also best not to plant a new rosebush where an old bush just died. They don't like used property. Rosarians refer to this as "rose soil sickness." I call it "bad juju." If that's your only area to plant a new rose, remove soil from an area that's at least 2 feet deep and 2 feet wide, and replace it with a fresh mixture of compost and clean soil, and don't let the new rose see what you're doing. She'll immediately call her agent and then I swear, your name will be mud.

When planting a new bare-root or a container rose, dig a hole at least 2 feet wide by 2 feet deep and create a center cone of the native soil to spread the roots onto. I hope you've amended this area with a top layer of compost in the last few months. (If you haven't, you can add compost or aged chicken manure into the hole and mix it into the native soil.) After the roots are covered and several shovelfuls of soil are placed in, fill the hole with water and let it drain. Then finish planting and water again.

If planting in Zone 7 and north, plant the bulbous center called the bud union (the heart of the rose) 1 to 3 inches below the soil level. If planting in Zone 8 and south, plant the bud union just above the soil line. Place a nice high mound of mulch around the newly planted rose, making sure to keep mulch from touching the stem. (You'll remove the mound of mulch in the spring when the weather warms up.) Let the winter and spring rains water your rosesbushes. After that, make sure you're watering them regularly, keeping the soil wet down to 18 inches.

Pruning Roses

Tools You Will Need

Pruning shears

Loppers (for large, thick canes that pruning shears won't get through)

Gloves

Guts

Here in California, I usually prune my 20-some rosebushes on New Year's morning. Being out in the fresh air works wonders for a cheap-Champagne-induced hangover. For those of you in colder climates, wait till late March or April. If you're new to growing roses and not sure when to prune, check with your local garden nursery. There's no foolproof answer for when to prune, but a good rule of thumb is to prune when dormancy is broken (you'll see new growth, especially budding eyes, which are red swollen dots on the major canes) and there's no threat of another hard freeze. Pruning roses helps speed up nature's growth cycle. It permits good air circulation and allows the plant to concentrate its energy on the remaining healthy shoots. If time permits, 2 weeks before you prune, gently remove all the leaves off of your rosebushes. Cutting them off works better than stripping and pulling. This will signal the plant to rejuvenate the foliar process. You'll also be able to see more clearly the swollen red eye, where new growth will form. This is where you will make your cut.

General Rose Pruning Steps

(Safety note: Always wear gloves.)

1. Remove any dead wood or old canes.
2. Cut out any weak, spindly, or deformed growth.
3. Remove any canes growing toward the center of the bush. (Aim to form an urn shape.)
4. Remove any suckers. (Undesired skinny shoots that grow up

near the bud union (the bulbous center of the rose), usually a slightly different foliage color. Suckers are losers and will drain energy away from the main canes.)

5. With the remaining canes, shorten them by cutting them back by one-third to one-half of their original length, making sure to cut on a diagonal, ¼ inch above an outward-facing budding eye.

Pruning Note

Severe pruning will produce fewer but showier blossoms. I like to prune moderately, which means that each rosebush is left with four to eight canes, about 24 inches high, with airy space in the center of

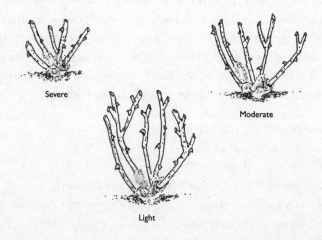

Severe

Moderate

Light

the bush. Light pruning will produce many blossoms on shorter stems. If you're new to pruning rosebushes, prune lightly the first year and see how you like it.

Last, there's always been some disagreement among rosarians about when to prune English roses and old roses: early winter or late summer? There's nothing more fun to watch than squabbling rosarians, is there? Most rose experts agree that modern roses and most English roses should be pruned in the late winter, whereas old roses should be pruned after they bloom in the summer. That's my story and I'm sticking to it. World renowned rosarian David Austin himself writes in his book *The English Roses*, "With relatively mild winters, late December to early February are the best times to prune. In regions with cold winters pruning should be delayed until spring growth is just starting."

It's also best not to prune old roses for the first three years and after that to prune lightly after bloom in the summer. Try it out and see what works best for you.

Climbing roses require only minimal pruning, if any at all, for the first few years. Just remove dead or spindly wood. After that, once the vigorous, mature climber starts taking over the neighborhood, don't be afraid to prune back many side shoots and a few main canes by half just to keep the shape and size from damaging your fence.

If the idea of pruning your roses is making you nervous, I'll let you in on a deep, dark rose secret: It will set you free. Pruning trials conducted by various rose societies consistently showed that rough pruning with a hedge trimmer produced results as good, or better, than traditional pruning methods. Take that, you hoity-toities! Take a deep breath and have faith you can do this. Once you get warmed up, you'll be unstoppable. Shazaam!

A FEW NOTEWORTHY REBLOOMING ROSES

Some roses have one springtime or summertime massive annual bloom, and some will bloom on and off throughout the growing season. It's good to have a bit of both types if you have the space. If not, choose the re-blooming type.

'**Bonica**' Easy, disease resistant; pink flowers that stay in bloom for many weeks.

'**Heritage**' British rosarian David Austin's favorite rose; honey-scented pink-ruffled cups.

'**Sally Holmes**' One of Amercian rosarian Rayford Reddell's favorites; pure flower factory of white to apricot blossoms.

'**Dainty Bess**' Party-girl rose; pink single petals of daisy-like blossoms.

'**New Dawn**' Light pink aggressive climber, can withstand some shade.

'**Cornelia**' Coral pink scented large flowers.

'**Iceberg**' Many white flowers all summer; great as a bush or climber; disease resistant.

'**Just Joey**' Perfect large apricot-scented blooms.

'**Altissimo**' Strong-growing; dark red, single-petaled climber; fragrance and good disease resistance. Can be grown as a large shrub or a climber.

'**Madame Alfred Carriere**' Faithful rebloomer; scented old-fashioned small white blossoms; aggressive climber.

Springtime Rose Care

When the danger of frost has passed in your area and leaflet sets begin to appear, this a sign that your roses are done loafing around and are calling their agents looking for work, demanding a good meal, and a stiff drink. They've just survived the cold, dank winter when they were basically neglected by you, and now they're back full throttle demanding attention. This is the time to gently unmound the layers of mulch you had surrounded your rosebushes with. Keep the mulch nearby. Spread it out a few inches away from the rose-bushes so that it continues to spread nutrients, conserve water, and control weeds. This is a good time to start feeding them alfalfa. You can buy a large bag of alfalfa pellets at a farm feed store to last you the entire year. (A 40-pound bag at the feed store can cost about $20.) Alfalfa is rich in nitrogen (5-1-2) and also releases a fatty acid growth stimulant called triacontanol. You'll want to scratch in 1 to 2 cups of alfalfa meal or pellets around the base of each large rosebush. If you'd rather not add alfalfa and have access to storybook farm animals, aged animal manure will make the roses giddy as well. Lightly rake a small amount of aged (has been sitting around for a few months) sheep, horse, turkey, or chicken manure around your roses.

When's Lunch?

Roses expend enormous energy in the production of growth and flowers. This can exhaust soil nutrients quickly. Here's a recipe rec-ommended by many rosarians. You can mix it up and feed about ½ cup per plant beginning in the spring and every month after through late summer. Work lightly into the soil and water thoroughly. You can find these ingredients at nurseries that have bins full of various min-erals and soil amendments or purchase organic products with these nutritious elements already in them.

2 parts bloodmeal or alfalfa meal

2 parts rock phosphate or bonemeal

1 part kelp meal

1 part Epsom salt (optional)

DON'T BE A CHUMP WARNING

It's best to water roses less frequently and very deep, than often and shallow. Never wet the leaves while watering. Use a soaker hose or drip system or hand water, avoiding any contact with the trunk or leaves. **Never ever** use a sprinkler on rosebushes, or rusty black spot will be your middle name. Watering in the morning is ideal so any moisture to the leaves can dry off before it encourages black spot or powdery mildew, two common fungal diseases. (In the hot summer, most rosebushes require 2 to 3 gallons of water two to three times a week. When watering, make sure you're soaking the ground at least 18 inches deep.)

SALTY NOTE

Use Epsom salt only when a rosebush is brand new and use it in moderation. The magnesium helps with the new root formation. After that, take it out of the mix. It's too salty and will accumulate in the soil over time, killing some microorganisms and decreasing the soil's water-holding capacity.

Evildoers That Get in the Way of Me Winning the Rose Contest at the County Fair

It's all fun and games growing roses until they get sick on you. If conditions have not been perfect: sun, drinks, organic food, and attention, they become susceptible to fungal diseases and insect infestations. Luckily these are all fairly common, and more and more environmentally safe products are coming on to the market to help combat rose problems. Don't fret or throw in the towel. Be patient and try to maintain a reasonable perspective on just how much damage a certain bug is presenting. Monitor the situation for a few days and see if you really must take action. Sometimes beneficial insects will swoop in and do the job for you before you must act. I've listed some of the most common rose evildoers and some suggestions to remedy the situation:

POWDERY MILDEW

Powdery mildew is recognized by its white powdery growth on leaves, shoots, and buds. Leaves may distort and drop. The fungus is active during warm, dry summers and will show up if plants are stressed from thirst. Simply keeping your rose waterings deep and consistent may solve this. Pruning, collecting, and disposing of leaves during the dormant season may limit infestations, but the spore is airborne. Glossy-foliaged varieties of hybrid teas and grandifloras often are more disease resistant. Plants grown in sunny locations with good air circulation are less likely to be infected. Commercial fungicides such as Garlic Pharm, Concern pesticidal oil, and E. B. Stone's copper soap have all shown good results to fight the fungus when applied at the correct time and consistently. Try this homemade recipe to keep it from spreading: Dissolve 1 tablespoon baking soda (which is alkaline), 1 tablespoon vegetable oil, and ½ teaspoon dishwashing detergent in 1 gallon water. Spray on leaves at first sign of trouble. Repeat a week later.

RUST

A fungus favored by cool and moist weather infects rose leaves, leaving small orange pustules. Leaves may drop and discolor. Avoid overhead watering and prune back severely any affected canes. In winter, dispose of any fallen leaves with rust. Be vigilant. Low levels of damage may be tolerated without great loss. Preventative applications of fungicides such as E. B. Stone's copper soap, Serenade's Garden

Disease Control, or Safer garden fungicide can be used but must be applied early enough to show any benefit.

BLACK SPOT
A fungus that produces black spots or fibrous margins on the upper surface of leaves and stems. The fungus requires water, so overhead watering should be avoided. Good air circulation is mandatory. The fungus starts in midsummer and is encouraged by the leaves staying wet for a few hours when the weather is warm. Remove all infected leaves and stems during the dormant season. Again a combination of a fungicide and a horticultural oil or neem oil has been shown to be effective for reducing black spot.

APHIDS
Aphids are the most common pests on roses. They thrive on actively growing tissue such as buds and shoots, so you'll find them often on roses just about to burst into bloom. They are the size of a pencil dot and can be brown or white. Although many novice gardeners panic when they first see the daunting sight of an aphid infestation, there really is no need to be concerned. Most rosebushes will be just fine by knocking aphids off with a forceful spray of water early in the day. Insecticidal soaps can also be used, but I have had great search-and-destroy success with a garden hose using a hard spray of water, and then repeating that satisfyingly vengeful method a few days later. Luckily for us, aphids have many natural enemies: lady beetles, soldier beetles, and syrphid flies. By keeping the use of toxic insecticides nonexistent in your yard, your garden has a better chance of attracting natural predators to enjoy the good life of feasting on your rose's aphids.

SPIDER MITES
Spider mites cause rose leaves to stipple and yellow. Often webbing may appear or leaves will dry up and fall. Spider mites are the size of

DID YOU KNOW?

"Stem Mothers" are the aphids that emerge from overwintering eggs in your garden in April. These plump babes do not need to mate. The sisterhood simply gives birth to live daughters, and these offspring give birth to more live daughters, all without males! It's a splendid all-girl world till late in the season, when some flirty aphid gets a hankering for a studmuffin. Then there are boy aphids born and the usual dating and mating shenanigans begin.

a dot or smaller. Insecticidal soap or horticultural oils have both shown good results, but you must remain vigilant. You may have to repeat applications once a week for a week or two. Invite these beneficial bugs to come eat mites: lady beetles, lacewing flies, big-eyed bugs, and pirate bugs. Plant yarrow, milkweed, asters, marigold, sages, and lavenders to attract these insect allies.

Cutting for a Bouquet

Rinse out a vase or pail with a mild solution of ammonia or white vinegar in water, to remove any bacteria. Then fill it up with warm water. Take along the container and pruning shears into the garden with you. (I like to take a pack of disinfectant wipes along as well, to wipe the pruning blade after each rose I cut so I don't spread any diseases to other roses.)

Rose leaves come in sets of three, five, and seven. Heirloom and some modern varieties produce nine or more leaflets. But all you need to remember is the number five. When cutting roses for a bouquet of flowers, always cut the stem at a point where you're leaving at least two sets of five leaflets on the rosebush stem. Make your cut ¼ inch above a five-leaflet set (that is facing outward from the center of the bush) on a diagonal. If all goes according to plan, in time, a new rose will grow from where you just cut.

Flowers go into shock when they're removed from their mother plant. Some rose growers suggest soaking them for 24 hours in water with bleach. This will help push away bacteria so the rose stem can take a proper drink. The bleach solution also allows the stem to take in the nutrients from a flower preservative (or sugar), which you can add later.

1. Carry your vase or pail of cut roses into the kitchen. Re-cut them again by ¼ inch under water in the kitchen sink. Remove lower leaves that would be in the water.
2. Place them in a container with hot water and bleach. (Only two to three drops per quart.)

3. Leave the container overnight in a dark, cool spot.

4. The next day, re-cut the stems again under water and place in a vase with 1 teaspoon flower preservative or sugar per quart of clean water.

FURTHER READING (WITH COLOR, GRAPHIC ROSE PORN PHOTOGRAPHY) TO INTOXICATE YOU

Growing Roses Organically, by Barbara Wilde (Rodale, 2002)

The English Roses, by David Austin (Studio, 2000)

The Rose Bible, by Rayford Reddell (Chronicle Books, 1998)

A PLANT RECOMMENDATION FROM THE
DIRT DIVA ROYAL HORTICULTURAL SOCIETY

Lavatera
COMMON NAME: mallow

I adore this perennial because it is closely related to the hollyhock family, a true cottage garden favorite, and because it comes into overflowing, spectacular full bloom right after the roses finish their spring show. *Lavatera* 'Barnsley' is a semi-evergreen shrub that grows to about 6 feet with sprays of wispy pale pink hollyhock-type flowers with deep pink centers, and is frost hardy. *L. thuringiaca* grows a foot shorter, and *Lavatera* 'Kew Rose' is a bit less frost hardy but has darker pink flowers. All are easy and perfect shrubs for a back of a border. They live only a few years, but they're easy to make cuttings from and they're extremely fast growers.

ORIGIN: Mediterranean region
HARDINESS: Zones 6–10
GROWING REQUIREMENTS: Plant in sun to part-sun after last frost in an area with some space. This plant will take off and arch gracefully with pink blossoms in early summer. You'll be so pleased with it. Likes moist, well-draining soil. Deadhead regularly for a longer summer bloom period.

THE UNIVERSAL BOTANICAL
WHAAA-WHAA RATING: **2**

17

Cut Flowers That'll Make Your Friends Weep

The choices for cut flowers are endless and include many flowering shrubs, perennials, annuals, vegetables, herbs, and even the seed heads or foliage of weeds. The best time to cut flowers is in the evening because sugar has been stored in the plant tissue all day. If you missed the boat on that slot, the next best time to cut flowers is early in the morning, before the dew has dried. This is when a plant contains the most water and its stems are full. The plants have spent the previous daylight hours manufacturing food for themselves, and the blossoms will be filled with nutrients to help them survive in the vase. The worst time of day to cut flowers is in the middle of the day. Shouldn't you be at work then? Or tweeting?

When growing cut flowers, I like to spread them out throughout my garden instead of having a cutting garden just in one area. Feel free to plant flowers in your vegetable beds as well. They all get along just fine and can even help invite insect allies to come eat the pests on your crops. And don't forget to give your flowers the care they need: water, soil amended with compost, some fertilizer (if they're loafing around), diligent weeding, a layer of mulch, and frequent deadheading—you shall be rewarded.

Making the Cut

First, clean off your vase with a mild solution of ammonia or white vinegar in water to get rid of any bacteria that has accumulated from your last bouquet. Rinse it well and fill it up with clean warm water. Take the vase, along with disinfected and sharp pruning shears, into the garden with you. Take your time, breathe, putter around a bit, be grateful for what Mother Nature has bestowed on you, and then get to cutting.

The general rule is to not cut tightly closed buds or mature flowers. Most flowers are best cut when the buds are half open. (Some exceptions are asters, mums, marigolds, and zinnias, which should be cut when they're fully open.) Whenever possible cut the stem above a node or the point where two stems meet, so that the plant will be able to send out a new shoot. After you make your cut, plunge the cut flower up to its neck into the warm water. It's even better to cut the flower stem again, indoors under tap water. My botanist friends swear that a second cutting, about 1 inch long, will extend the vase life. So go for the second cut. When flowers are out of water for even a short time, their stems seal off. Re-cutting them lets them draw up water again. It's best to cut stems on a slant so that the water-conducting cells are in contact with water even when the ends are sitting on the bottom of a vase.

Flowers that bleed a milky sap or clear fluid bleed out nutrients that attract bacteria. For these flowers, it's good to quickly dip the cut end of the stems in boiling hot water. Some such flowers are campanula, daffodil, hollyhock, forget-me-not, hydrangea, lantana, Oriental poppy, lobelia, dahlia, and zinnia. If you need a cheap thrill and are part pyromaniac, you can pass the tip of these flowers into a flame momentarily, instead of hot water. Fire it up! Many flowers will last longer if you scrape the bottom inch of the stem with a knife or your clippers to expose a greater surface to the water. These flowers are happy with a little scraping: anemone, aster, bachelor button, calendula, daisy, daffodil, delphinium, gladiola, iris, lilac, marigold, peony, rose, and tulip.

When arranging flowers, remove any leaves that would be underwater in the vase and make sure to leave good air circulation. Fill the vase with clean, lukewarm water (very hot or cold water will shock the flowers). Adding a preservative can prolong the life of some cut flowers by 200 percent! You can make your own preservative by adding 3 tablespoons of sugar and 1 tablespoon alum to 1 gallon of water or simply by adding one aspirin to the water in your vase. (Another method I've heard works wonders is to mix 1 part regular lemon-lime soda [not diet soda] with 3 parts warm water. Better in a vase than on your kid's teeth.)

If possible, let your bouquet condition, or "harden," by leaving the vase in a dark room for a couple of hours or overnight. Conditioning flowers closes their stomata (tiny openings in the leaves and stems) so they lose less water by transpiration, which helps your arrangement last longer. Add fresh water to the vase every day or every other day. After a few days, change all of the water, toss out any spent flowers and add a fresh preservative. Lightly misting the bouquet whenever you remember will also help extend the life of your arrangement.

If you're taking a bouquet to a friend's house to impress them (why else have friends?), wrap the stems in a wet paper towel and put the stems or the entire bouquet in a plastic bag. Keep it out of the sun during travel. When you arrive, re-cut the stems under water and place into a clean vase.

Though annual flowers are the mainstay of a good cutting garden, here are some other options that make a dramatic statement in a fresh cut-flower arrangement.

TREE BRANCHES

MAPLE *(ACER)* The leaves and graceful branches provide stunning color mostly in the fall, and some varieties all year round. A nice combination is red maple leaves with a few pale pink peonies.

DOGWOOD *(CORNUS)* The variety *C. alba* 'Sibirica' has red stems that are long lasting in an arrangement.

CHERRY *(PRUNUS)* In early spring, before the leaves appear, pink or white slightly fragrant flower blossoms steal the show on graceful branches.

SHRUBS

BUTTERFLY BUSH *(BUDDLEIA)* Fragrant blossoms and naturally curving stems make this an excellent addition to a tall flower arrangement in the summer months. (Cut branches when half the flowers are open.)

LILAC *(SYRINGA)* Pink to purple scented flower stems mixed with some of their own green leaves, in a white pitcher, make a gorgeous arrangement.

EUCALYPTUS These branches provide contrasting gray foliage and do well in dried or fresh flower arrangements.

VIBURNUM These shrubs will give you small white flowers as well as winter berries and distinctive foliage.

RHODODENDRON AND AZALEA *(RHODODENDRON)* Both of these plants are filled with fine materials for flower arranging.

PERENNIALS

Although there are too many perennials to list them all, here are some top performers that share the ability to retain their freshness indoors for a few days and make you seem quite Martha Stewart-esque.)

Anemone	Dahlia	Phlox
Aster	Echinacea	Poppy
Baby's breath	Gaillardia	Rose
Black-eyed Susan	Gladiola	Salvia
Columbine	Hollyhock	Shasta daisy
Coralbells	Iris	Tulip
Coreopsis	Lavender	Yarrow
Daffodil	Peony	

ANNUALS

Bachelor button	Larkspur	Stock
Calendula	Love-in-a-mist	Sunflower
Cosmos	Marigold	Sweet pea
Forget-me-not	Scabiosa	Verbena
Foxglove	Snapdragon	Zinnia
Godetia	Statice	

VEGETABLES

Artichoke	Mustard	Scarlet runner bean

HERBS

Anise	Chive	Pineapple sage
Artemisia	Garlic	Rosemary
Borage	Lavender	Sage
Chamomile	Lemon verbena	Sorrel

Sunflowers make fantastic cut flowers.

Last, while we're on the topic of bouquets, did you know that most commercially grown, fresh cut flowers that you buy at the florist or supermarket are sprayed with an artillery of toxic fertilizers, insecticides, and fungicides? These chemicals don't just deplete the soil and contaminate the environment but also poison the farmworkers who grow the flowers. Many of these chemicals are tightly restricted in the United States because of their threat to human health. About 70 percent of all flowers sold in the United States are grown in Colombia and Ecuador. Next time you're sending a bouquet to an out-of-town pal, consider ordering from Organic Bouquet (www.organicbouquet .com), the world's first online organic florist. Purchasing fresh flowers for our dining room tables while poisoning farmers and their families is so *yesterday*!

THREE TECHNIQUES THAT CAN HELP IMPROVE FLOWER PRODUCTION IN YOUR YARD

1. **Pinching:** This can be applied to plants like stock and snapdragons. Pinch or remove the growing tips when the plant is still young so it becomes bushier. This can easily be done by nipping out the end bud or small new leaves with your fingertips.

2. **Disbudding:** If a plant has many buds, you can remove a few of them. You'll have fewer flowers but larger ones.

3. **Deadheading:** Remove spent flowers or simply cut flowers for a bouquet. This way you're stimulating the plant to form more flowers. This works well on marigolds, daisies, pansies, sweet peas, and many others.

Chrysanthemum × superbum
COMMON NAME: Shasta daisy

Shasta daisies make excellent cut flowers. Many years ago my husband became obsessed with growing Shasta daisies. We were novice gardeners at the time and the only thing that grew easily in our yard was this daisy. Just like you don't mess with a sleeping baby, you don't mess with plants that are thriving in your yard. You find out what they are and plant more!

These 3-foot-tall perennials have glistening white petals with yellow centers and can easily be divided every fall or early spring to form new plants. In the fall, cut foliage to the ground.

ORIGIN: China, Japan, Europe
HARDINESS: Zones 5–9
GROWING REQUIREMENTS: Grow in full sun or partial shade if summers are very hot in nutrient-rich, well-drained soil. (Though you may need to stake plants in the shade.) They require low to regular water and will droop on extremely hot days but recover by nightfall. They attract butterflies, bees, and birds and are deer resistant.

THE UNIVERSAL BOTANICAL
WHAAA–WHAA RATING: **2**

18
Butterflies in the 'Hood

Butterflies, those graceful insects from the Lepidoptera family, are not only enchanting show-stoppers but are essential pollinators of plants and a critical food source for a variety of animals. Unfortunately, our national ignorance of using broad-spectrum pesticides in home gardening practices has caused a dramatic decline in butterfly populations. Some species are already extinct and several others are endangered.

Attracting Butterflies to Your Yard

Flowers that butterflies enjoy visiting are rich in nectar. Butterflies prefer a mass of colorful, diverse, fragrant flowers preferably with tubular or flat, upright blossoms. Like any true sun-worshiping attention stealer, they also request a perching spot in their contract. They love a big rock or evergreen in your garden that they can sit on in the early morning and a warm, sheltered area, where they're protected from wind. Butterflies can fly only if their body temperature is above

86°F. They'll sit and sun themselves on a nice warm rock to heat up their internal motor before they take to the air. The fastest ones can fly about 30 miles per hour. The slowpokes fly 5 mph. A sunny location will help attract more butterflies and will also help produce more butterflies. The warmth of the sun can also help young caterpillars develop more rapidly, sometimes up to 50 percent.

Butterflies even have favorite colors: yellow, pink, orange, and purple. And luckily for us, they're not neat freaks. They'd rather visit a more natural, less perfect garden than an orderly one as long as it's filled with many, many flowers.

Metamorphosis 101

A male and female butterfly mate. This can take from 10 minutes to several hours and sometimes is achieved while flying in midair. (Say what!) Tiny eggs are then usually laid on a leaf. They'll hatch in about a week. The larva (caterpillar) hatches and eats your garden leaves and flowers for a few weeks. (A good reason not to spray *all* caterpillars, thinking they are pests.) The larva will shed its skin four to six times and then transform into a pupa. This is when the larva's body soon turns into a beautiful butterfly. The pupa or chrysalis stage is its growing and resting time. A monarch butterfly will pupate for roughly 10 days, while a pipeline swallowtail can chill for months.

BUTTERFLY ANATOMY

Adult butterflies eat by sipping nectar from flowers with their tube-like long, flexible tongue. In case you thought butterflies were graceful and refined, forget about that. Some drink the bodily fluids of aphids. Larvae, on the other hand, have chewing mouthparts that they use to skeletonize or defoliate leaves. Butterflies have large, rounded compound eyes that allow them to see in all directions without turning their heads. Like most insects, butterflies are nearsighted and are more attracted to large stands of a particular flower than those planted singly. They don't see red as well as we do, but they can see polarized light (which tells them the direction the sun is pointing) as well as ultraviolet light, which is present on many flowers. This guides them to nectar sources. They also have a well-developed sense of smell from their antennae.

INVITE THEM OVER

A caterpillar host plant is the plant that adult butterflies will use for egg laying. Many species of butterflies will lay their eggs on only one or a few types of plants, while others are less selective. The concerned and doting mama butterfly will place her eggs on plants she knows her emerging newborns will eat. Hollyhock, thistle, and mallow are all host plants for the painted lady butterfly. Milkweed is a host plant for Monarch butterflies.

COMMON PLANTS THAT A VARIETY OF CATERPILLARS CAN FEED ON

Alfalfa (*Medicago sativa*)	Grasses, sedges
Aspen, cottonwood (*Populus*)	Hackberry (*Celtis*)
Cabbage, broccoli (*Brassica*)	Milkweed (*Asclepias*)
Cherry (*Prunus*)	Queen Anne's lace (*Daucus carota*)
Clover (*Trifolium*)	
Dutchman's-pipe (*Aristolochia*)	Vetch (*Vicia*)
False Nettle (*Boehmeria cylindrica*)	Violet (*Viola*)
	Wildflowers

TOP NECTAR PLANTS FOR ADULT BUTTERFLIES

Aster (*Aster*)	Buckeye tree (*Aesculus*)
Black-eyed Susan (*Rudbeckia*)	Butterfly weed (*Asclepias tuberosa*)

Butterfly bush (*Buddleia*)

Coreopsis (*Coreopsis*)

Cosmos (*Cosmos*)

Joe-pye weed (*Eupatorium*)

Lantana (*Lantana camara*)

Liatris (*Liatris*)

Mexican sunflower (*Tithonia*)

Milkweed (*Asclepias*)

Purple coneflower (*Echinacea purpurea*)

Red valerian (*Centranthus*)

Sunflower (*Helianthus*)

Tree mallow (*Lavatera*)

Yarrow (*Achillea*)

and . . . yes, weeds

MEET THE BUTTERFLY CONTESTANTS

What's for lunch? Here are some of the most common butterflies and their favorite foods:

Blues Adult butterflies like to munch on mustards, clovers, and asters, while the kids want legumes and cover crops like vetch, clover, and alfalfa.

Coppers and Metalmarks Adult butterflies enjoy white clover, yarrow, and butterfly weed, while the kids like sheep sorrel, curled dock, and wild buckwheat.

Fritillaries Adults request black-eyed Susans, daisies, and clovers, while kids like violets.

Hairstreaks Adults feed on weedy, short-tubed flowers such as mustards, mints, and milkweeds, while the kids like to visit the legumes, mallows, blueberries, and oaks.

Longwings Adults enjoy tropical forests and lantana. The larvae crave passion flowers.

Painted Ladies, Red Admiral, and Buckeye Most adults prefer open spaces with low vegetation and a variety of flowers, while kids want snapdragons, thistles, hollyhock, borage, and mallows.

PUDDLE CLUBS

Another way to attract butterflies to your yard is by creating puddles. Butterflies are often seen on the side of a dirt road or a path where there's recently been puddles created by rain. They like to come for a visit and drink up the remaining concentrated minerals. When butterflies are puddling, they're so absorbed in chow-time that this is a great time to get very close and even pick one up briefly. To create your own puddle club, fill a bowl with wet sand and sink it in the ground or simply make a small puddle in a sunny corner of your garden. If mosquitoes come to breed instead, get rid of it and don't call me. I'm busy watching *Seinfeld* reruns.

Milkweed Butterflies (Monarch and Queens) Adults want taller flowers and a mass of blooms; they also like a field of wildflowers such as asters, goldenrod, and thistle. The kids whine for common milkweed or butterfly weed.

Swallowtails Adults like tall tubular flowers, while the kids will be attracted by pipevine, fennel, carrot, dill, bay trees, citrus trees, and stonecrops.

Whites Adults and kids like wide open meadows and enjoy laying their eggs on mustard plant leaves (cabbage, broccoli, pepper grass, mustard).

Skippers Adults and kids prefer fields, grasses, legumes, and a well-rounded variety of nectar plants.

Sulfurs Adults are attracted to wildflowers, while the kids like marigolds and a vegetable garden, preferably with plants of the legume family such as peas or beans. The larvae also enjoy cover crops of alfalfa, vetch, and clover.

Snout and Hackberry All like hackberry trees and rotted fruit. What a bunch of hacks!

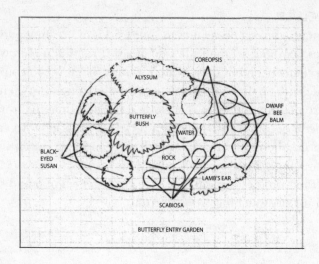

A simple butterfly plot filled with nectar plants. Visit the Butterfly Site (www.thebutterflysite .com) to see which types of butterflies hang in your 'hood.

FOR MORE ABOUT BUTTERFLIES

Stokes Beginners Guide to Butterflies, by Donald Stokes, Lillian Stokes (Little, Brown and Company, 2001)

A PLANT RECOMMENDATION FROM THE
DIRT DIVA ROYAL HORTICULTURAL SOCIETY

Buddleia
COMMON NAME: butterfly bush

Buddleia davidii (named after botanist Adam Buddle), the common
butterfly bush of gardens, can grow to 12 feet with its arching
canes bearing long, narrow cones of tiny deep purple or mauve
flowers at their tips. Butterflies feed on the scented nectar
throughout the summer. Can be prone to aphids,
budworm, and earwigs chewing the leaves. (Buddleia
'Ellen's Blue', with its gray-green foliage, seems to be less
attractive to the pernicious leaf-chewing budworm.) Cut back
in early spring to its ankles.

ORIGIN: China
HARDINESS: Zones 5–10
GROWING REQUIREMENTS: Full sun or light shade, amended soil,
and moderate watering.

THE UNIVERSAL BOTANICAL
WHAAA–WHAA RATING: **4**

19

Pruning, Dividing, Cutting, and Running

All shrubs and perennials require a certain amount of pruning about once a year if only to remove dead wood or a damaged branch. Why prune? Pruning stimulates the growth of new shoots and helps keep plants healthy and prolific. For novice gardeners, pruning can be a nerve-wracking and insecure time, filled with trepidation and angst. And guilt. That's okay. You and your plants will live to tell. Plants are much more resilient than they let on. They like you to think they're delicate and need constant hand-holding, but for the most part, that's untrue. They're faking it. Most are quite independent, you'll learn. It's just like those first few days of dropping your toddler off at pre-school so you can go to work or have a life. You leave that sweet crying child in the classroom and you run out the door weeping yourself, feeling incredibly guilty. You sniffle away down the sidewalk like a sappy pathetic new parent, wondering if you should go back in, but then, only a few minutes later, you drive past the classroom window and that crying baby is smiling and laughing, perched on the teacher's lap, clapping. What a faker! That's exactly

TOOLS YOU MAY NEED

Gloves
Pruners (for thin stems)
Loppers (for thick wood)
Hand shears (for hedges)
Tree pruners (for fruit trees; pruners on a long pole)
Electric hedge trimmer (if you have lots of hedges and ... cuz it's fun!)

what your plants are doing when you walk away mortified with those pruners in your hand. They're laughing and clapping.

Shrubs

A good time to prune many shrubs is in the early spring because the leaves are off of the plant and you can see any dead or diseased branches. Wondering what dead wood looks like? It looks like *dead* wood. If not sure, cut a small piece and see if there is any green color inside. If no green appears, take a deep breath and cut off the dead wood as close to the larger stem as possible. Then cut off any branches that cross or rub on another branch.

Flowering shrubs are usually divided into two categories determined by when they form flower buds. At first it's a bit confusing, but you'll soon become familiar with which plant to prune when. Because there are so many exceptions to every garden rule ever made, even we Master Gardeners have to check our pruning books from time to time. It's good to keep a notebook with dates. That way you can con-

DON'T BE A CHUMP WARNING

Even though it's tempting, don't prune during PMS or after a long, wearisome phone call with your mother or immediately after a divorce. You'll regret your severe slashing and then you'll have more to sob about. Put away the sharp objects and go get a pint of Ben and Jerry's Chunky Monkey instead.

tact me with proof and try to make me feel bad for making you chop off all the buds from your grandmother's prized hydrangea.

In general, *spring-flowering* plants can be pruned once the flowers fade and new growth starts. Most often this will be in summer. (These flowers form buds on the previous year's growth, so if you pruned them in the early spring, you'd be cutting off many of the flowers.) Some of these are lilac, quince, and forsythia.

Most *summer-* and *fall-flowering* plants will produce flower buds on the new growth produced in the same season, so you can prune them in the late winter, during the dormant season. Sometimes it means pruning a plant to the ground or a foot from the ground in March. Be brave. (*Buddleia davidii* is a good example.)

Always prune from the bottom up and from the inside of the plant to the outside. Starting from the bottom will help you notice any diseased lower branches that don't get much light and tend to die. Get rid of them. Look for an outward-facing bud or leaflet and prune right above that on a slant.

SOME SHRUB AND PERENNIAL PRUNING SUGGESTED GUIDELINES

Flowering Maple *(Abutilon)* Cut back branches 6 to 12 inches in the spring just above a bud.

Butterfly Bush *(Buddleia)* Varieties vary, but the most common, *B. davidii*, should be cut back to the ankles in early spring.

Campanula Shear back to basal foliage after bloom in summer.

Cardinal Flower *(Lobelia cardinalis)* Good to leave alone through the winter and prune back to the ground in early spring.

Currant, Flowering *(Ribes sanguineum)* Cut out the oldest one-third of the shoots in spring after flowering to prevent the plant from becoming too leggy.

Coralbells *(Heuchera)* Leave foliage on through the winter and prune back in early spring. These are extremely fast growers, so prune back severely if it's getting too big.

Cushion Spurge Cut back to the base in early spring.

Daphne These sweet-smelling flowers actually require no routine pruning, but you can cut out straggly shoots in early spring just to keep it tidy.

Foxglove *(Digitalis purpurea)* Prune back the stalks a bit after it blooms in summer and you may get another bloom. After that, prune back to the base.

Hydrangea *(Hydrangea macrophylla)* On mopheads and lacecaps, leave the old brown flower heads on the plant during the winter months to help protect the flower buds from frost damage. (I know, they look miserable. Get used to it!) In early spring, when you see green growth, remove the old flower heads.

Hosta Prune back in early spring.

Jasmine (*Jasminum*) Most can be cut back hard in early spring. Very hardy and will come back fierce!

Lamb's Ears (*Stachys byzantina*) Remove winter damage when the leaves come up in the spring.

Lavender (*Lavendula*) Sensitive to cold, so leave old foliage on through the winter. You can deadhead lightly after summer bloom and prune back to the base in the early spring to encourage a bushy habit.

Lilac Evergreen types simply need deadheading (remove spent blossoms) after bloom, while deciduous varieties can be cut back harder to within 3 buds of the previous year's growth.

Oriental Poppy (*Papaver orientale*) Poppies can be pruned back to the base in early spring.

Pincushion Flower (*Scabiosa*) Prune back to the base after summer flowering.

Plumbago Deadhead after summer flowering in most climates.

Purple Coneflower (*Echinacea purpurea*) Prune back to the base after summer flowering.

Rhododendron None required but gently deadheading after bloom will make it look tidy and put energy into new buds. If necessary, remove dead wood from center to allow better air circulation.

Russian Sage (*Perovskia atriplicifolia*) Leave alone for the winter and prune back to 6 inches from the ground in early spring.

Sedum Leave alone in the winter. Prune back to base in the spring.

Tree Mallow (*Lavatera*) In early spring cut back one-third of stalks to just above soil level and cut remaining stalks to 1 to 2 feet tall. I promise it will come back fuller and happier.

Wandflower (*Gaura*) Can prune to the ground in the fall and watch it bounce back in the spring.

DIVIDING

Most perennials will need to be divided every 2 to 3 years to stay healthy. As a plant expands, the middle portion becomes crowded and hungry for nutrients, moisture, and light. Another reason to divide plants is that they may be growing too wide for the area you planted them in. This happened to me often as a novice gardener. I had little faith that the plant would actually grow to fill the area it was planted in so I planted them too close to the next. My husband, Bill, claims that it's because I grew up in a Manhattan apartment building where people live on top of each other, smothering one another with loud opinions and no escape hatch or breathing space. "That's why you unconsciously plant flowers in an overcrowded, abrasive, and asphyxiating style . . ." See, marriage can be *fun*!

Mostly you'll want to divide your plants because it's cheapskate horticulture: free plants. When opportunity knocks, you better answer the door. Or at least ask who's there. The optimum time to divide plants is when they're dormant. The best time to divide plants in colder climates is in the early spring when plants are still partially dormant. They're resting and clueless, so they'll suffer less shock then. They'll also have plenty of time to establish themselves in their new area before the winter freeze comes back around. In warmer climates, the general rule of thumb is to divide spring- and summer-blooming perennials in early fall, and fall bloomers in early spring. (Although once again, there are plenty of exceptions.)

Steps to Division

Choose an overcast day and don't stress out when dividing plants. Healthy plants are more adaptable than they let on and can survive a pretty lame hack job. (I promise your plants are not calling you the angel-of-death behind your back. Or are they? Only the bridge trolls know for sure.)

1. First, prepare the hole or a few holes where the newly divided plants will land.

2. Though there are some exceptions, most plants do best when the entire plant is dug out of the ground. Dig your shovel vertically underground 6 to 12 inches deep. Dig wide and deep with your shovel, and dig out the whole clump. Take your time and be ready for some underground resistance.

3. With your hands or with the sharp edge of the shovel, pull or cut apart the tight roots of the clump into sections. Aim to create two to four new plants from the original plant. Some perennials are difficult to divide. If so, place plant on the ground, lying on its side, and stab it with the tip of your shovel, breaking the plant into two to four clumps. Apologize later.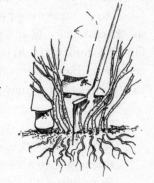

4. Plant these new clumps in their new spot. Water and pamper them for a bit.

Note: More experienced gardeners do not remove the entire plant from the ground when dividing. They're fear-

A Few Easy Plants to Divide

Agapanthus	Monarda
Alstroemeria	Phlox
Gaillardia	Certain salvias
Geranium	Sedum
Heuchera	Shasta daisy
Hosta	Stachys
Lily-of-the-valley	

less and busy showing off. They simply take the shovel and slice half of the plant off down to its roots, and plant the new clump. This works fine, especially if the entire plant is too heavy and stubborn to lift out of the ground.

CUTTINGS

Cuttings are cut sections of a living plant that will develop a root system once in the ground. Why take cuttings? To have more free plants of course. Some woody plants can't be divided but can have a cutting taken to create another plant. The best time to take stem cuttings in most areas is spring and early summer, but I've taken cuttings in the fall (in California) and have had success. It's also best not to take cuttings from blooming plants because the plant's energy is going into the blooms, so they may not root as well.

Steps to Soft-Wood Cuttings

1. Collect cuttings early in the day on a cool morning. Using a sharp and clean knife or shears, snip a 5- to 6-inch-long stem from the plant, cutting just below a node (the swelling where the leaves emerge). If all goes according to plan (ha!), new roots will form from this node.

2. Next, pinch off any flowers. Then pinch or cut off all leaves from the lower part of the stem, leaving only the top two to four leaves.

3. Cuttings will have faster success if placed in a container with good drainage filled with a commercial potting mix and humid air. Dip ¼ inch of the stem into a powdered- or gel-type rooting compound, which is inexpensive and can be found at nurseries. Then, with a pencil, make a 1- to 2-inch-deep hole in the dampened growing mix. Insert the stem into the hole, letting the stem sit on the potting mix. (The cutting should have about a third of its length under the growing mix.) Pat it down so

there are no air pockets. Then label your cuttings with dates and names.

4. Place each potted cutting into a clear plastic bag and loosely tie the bag shut at the top of the plant, letting in some air. This will create a humid environment for good rooting. (You can place a chopstick in the soil, near the stem, to keep the plastic off of the plant.)

5. Set the containers in a bright spot indoors or out, but out of direct sun. Open the bag occasionally for an hour or two to let in air. Mist cutting if it's looking homesick away from the mothership.

Most cuttings root in 2 to 5 weeks. You'll want to see some new growth and roots before you gently remove the plastic and transplant cuttings into larger pots or out in the yard.

Plant-in-a-bubble note: If the plastic bag part seems too time-consuming, leave it out, but you'll have to mist the leaves on your cutting consistently. Check the moisture daily if possible.

10 PLANTS TO EASILY PROPAGATE FROM CUTTINGS

Aster	*Lavatera*
Buddleia	Lavender
Catmint	Lion's tail
Dianthus	Penstemon
Geranium	Salvia

A PLANT RECOMMENDATION FROM THE
DIRT DIVA ROYAL HORTICULTURAL SOCIETY

Stachys byzantina
COMMON NAME: lamb's ears

This low-maintenance and easy to divide perennial ground cover got its common name from its fuzzy leaves that have the velvety feel of a lamb. Stachys is from the mint family, so it can get invasive, but I like having lots of them around, since they're drought tolerant and attract butterflies and bees. The variety 'Big Ears' bears tall spikes of purple flowers in the summer. 'Silver Carpet' rarely flowers. *S. coccinea* is a U.S. native that blooms in the summer with bright red flowers that are irresistible to hummingbirds. All varieties of *Stachys* work well as a border plant. Place plants from 4-inch containers, 1 to 2 feet apart, and they'll fill in rapidly.

ORIGIN: Iran
HARDINESS: Zones 5–10
GROWING REQUIREMENTS: It does best in sun and doesn't like wet conditions. The leaves will turn mushy in cold, wet, or humid weather but will recover. Drought tolerant.

THE UNIVERSAL BOTANICAL
WHAAA–WHAA RATING: **1**

PART FOUR

Edible Gardening

In Chapter 20, "Cover Crops: Soil Building Without Lifting a Finger," I explain why you, too, will become a fan of cover crops. These are exceptional seeds you sow in the soil when a section of your garden is taking a well-deserved siesta. This is how organic farmers build their soil to grow food year after, when their land lies fallow. If they can grow fields and fields in this safe and sustainable manner, trust me, you can grow a raised bed of edible crops without polluting your entire ZIP code with chemical fertilizers.

In Chapter 21, "Grow Your Own," you'll have new admiration for farmers when you see the daily challenges they deal with throughout the year. When it comes to growing vegetables, careful planning and consistent watering and watching are key. This will help your crops prosper and actually look somewhat like the picture on the seed package.

If you don't have time or space for a full-blown edible garden, follow the advice in Chapter 22, "Herb Gardens." Herbs are the easiest, least-demanding edible plants to grow. They also deter many pests with their strong, fabulous fragrance.

If you're up for a challenge, read Chapter 23, "Return of the Killer Tomatoes." Here I share with you how to outperform your sister's legendary homegrown tomatoes, organically. Enough of her showing off! If you've got hot sun and can water consistently, you can grow tomatoes without worrying too much about common pests and disease.

In Chapter 24, "Flowers Good Enuf to Eat," you'll find out which plants are edible and which are poisonous and how you can mix edible flowers into your overall landscape design. When your family starts seeing salads made with nasturtiums, calendulas, and violas on top, they'll suspect you're planning your escape, and they'll start being really, really sweet. Milk it for as long as you can.

Last, in Chapter 25, "Fruit Tree Helper," I try to answer all those questions that home gardeners wonder about. Should I fertilize fruit trees? When do I prune them? Do I have to spray them in the winter? Most fruit trees are surprisingly simple to grow, and they're a sensible investment for your yard. Many homeowners are pulling out their ornamental plants and replacing them with more edibles, especially fruit trees. How can you say no to a pineapple guava tree?! (*Feioja*, Zones 9–11.) You can't!

20
Cover Crops

SOIL BUILDING WITHOUT LIFTING A FINGER

I f you're going to grow food in your garden, learning when and how to use cover crops is essential. These crops can be grown for flower gardens as well, so if you're not growing vegetables, read up on how you can use these simple seeds even in the ornamental parts of your yard.

Growing cover crops (also called green manure) is the easiest way to add nutrients to your soil while making your garden look prolific and lush instead of fallow and futile during the winter months. Letting my garden rest during the dormant season just doesn't cut it for me. I need to know that everyone around me is multitasking 24/7. Cover crops do five remarkable things for the home gardener: They add nutrients to the soil, their flowers invite beneficial insects, they protect the soil from erosion, they compete and smother weeds, and they improve the soil's tilth (physical condition). And, they do all this while looking fabulous! Organic farmers grow cover crops in orchards and fields, planting them in the fall so they nourish the land before they plant their warm-season commercial crops.

The organic matter provided when you plow under a cover crop months after planting it will improve soil structure and aeration, increase water and nutrient-holding capacity, and supply a portion of the nutrient requirements for whatever you're planting next. In October of each year, I sow a pound or two of cover crop seeds in my vegetable garden and around perennial beds that in the past have been filled with weeds after the winter rains and neglect. This way, when my garden is dormant throughout the winter, it's actually doing something useful instead of just sitting there complaining, "You said this would be fun," "Why can't we watch TV?" and "I hate nature. I want an iPhone!"

Depending on your climate zone, you can plant cover crops in the spring and summer as well, but the fall/winter crop is said to be the most critical for long-term soil health. Your soil and all the micro-workers under the ground will thank you as they supply nutrients, and you'll be spending less money on fertilizers. Don't just do it one year and say, okay, that was nice. Plan to do it every fall and or spring; like flossing your teeth, it should become a habit. (You don't floss just twice a year, before your cleaning. Or do you?) You can't just build your soil one year and then stop. Soil building is an ongoing process. This way you won't have to work so hard to keep your garden standing strong and healthy, and you can focus all your attention back on yourself. Hello? All roads lead back to *me*, should be your new mantra.

Let's Get Started

Don't try to find cover crops in those chain stores that have a so-called garden section that smells and looks more like a chemical warfare arsenal. They may not want home gardeners to know that they can actually fertilize their soil naturally for the price of a Venti latte, throughout the winter, by sprinkling a few seeds. But if that store is your only local option, you can educate them and ask them to order cover crops for you. (Then take a picture of the expression on their face and email it to me.) Check with your local independent plant nursery, or you can order a wonderful assortment of cover crop seeds online at Seeds of Change (www.seedsofchange.com) and Peaceful Valley Farm and Garden Supply (www.groworganic.com).

Some cover crops are sold in a packaged mix of grasses and legumes combined, and many are not edible so don't eat them! You're growing these crops to add organic matter to your soil so you can grow spectacular edible crops afterward. (If you're planting a few legumes to eat, such as fava beans or soybeans, purchase them individually at a nursery in a small seed pack or ask the supplier if they're safe to consume.)

STEP 1. Purchase seeds that are fresh and labeled for the current year. A 1-pound bag sells for about $2 to $8 depending on what the seeds are. Some organic nurseries have bins filled with peas, barley, buckwheat, and so on, and you can fill a bag with your choice of seeds; some nurseries have a premade mix of crops. (You'll want roughly ¼ pound of seed per 100 square feet of planting area.)

STEP 2. Broadcast seeds over clean soil that has been amended with compost and that's free of weeds. Lightly rake in. In about 2 weeks you should see seedlings popping up. (These seeds are very easy to establish outdoors in garden soil, compared to seeds that crave a fancy planting mix, so have no fear about them not sprouting.)

STEP 3. Cover crops are low maintenance, but they still need some care. Make sure they are watered consistently if there is no rain. You can cover them with straw or a thin layer of leaves to keep them cozy.

STEP 4. Let them grow for 6 weeks to a few months, but before they set seed, you'll have to turn under your crop. This is hard to do when they're just beginning to have beautiful flowers, but this is the time when the largest amount of nitrogen and organic matter is supplied. After that time, green manure production decreases and those cover crops you grew to increase soil fertility are just another pretty face. Who needs *that*? You want free fertilizer! If your cover crops are planted in the ground, you can mow them with your lawn mower. If they're in raised beds, as most of mine are, you can use a weed trimmer, or you can chop them up with hand pruners. I usually take my pruners or hedge shearers and chop the entire plant to the ground and then cut the fallen pieces into halves or quarters and leave then lying on top.

STEP 5. Wait a few days until the leaves and stems are dry and then dig them lightly into the soil. (Too much tilling can undo some of the soil benefit that you just supplied, so be gentle.) It's best to wait 3 weeks to a month for all the vegetative growth to decompose before adding new plants or seeds for your springtime flower or vegetable garden.

NITROGEN FIXERS

Cover crops from the legume family are said to fix nitrogen. These nitrogen stalkers magically capture and convert atmospheric nitrogen gas into nitrogen compounds. Don't ask me how it's done. I'm not a soil scientist. But, if you science-geeks must know: There's bacteria present on the nodules of the roots of many legume plants. This compelling bacteria pulls in atmospheric nitrogen and stores it in the soil. When the plant dies, its roots release the stored nitrogen. Ta-da!

LET'S MEET OUR CONTESTANTS

You may want to do some local research with other gardeners or nurseries or online to see which cover crops will thrive and be most beneficial or beautiful in your climate zone. If you're looking for something pretty and girly, as I'm prone to do, consider hairy vetch and fava beans. Here are some proven winners. Feel free to mix and match.

ALFALFA The king of soil building. A perennial legume that will fix nitrogen and also break up hard soil with its deep roots. Doesn't like wet growing conditions and needs warm temperatures for germinating.

ALSIKE CLOVER A biennial legume that enjoys poorly drained soil and does best in the northern states. Deep taproots loosen subsoil.

CRIMSOM CLOVER A legume with stunning deep red flowers. Slightly drought tolerant and a good soil builder. Also adds nitrogen and organic matter.

BUCKWHEAT Nonleguminous; unsurpassed for rebuilding poor, neglected soil; attracts beneficial insects and increases phosphorus and potassium availability. Vigorous top growth and massive root system make it an organic matter rock star!

COWPEA Fast-growing annual legume improves aeration and brings subsoil minerals up to the top.

OATS Nonleguminous; will germinate well in cool, moist conditions except clay. This is a quick grower ready to compete with weeds. Does well in northern climates.

FAVA BEANS One of my favorites; medium drought tolerance; likes cool weather. Excellent nitrogen fixer, and purty, purty purple flowers.

RED CLOVER An overachieving legume that accumulates phosphorus, grows quickly, attracts beneficials, suppresses weeds, and has pretty little red flowers.

RYE (ANNUAL OR WINTER) Hardy; withstands cold weather; will improve soil structure while adding organic matter. *Annual:* highly rated and considered one of the most valuable nonleguminous cover crops. Wait until the stalks are 10 inches high before you plow them under. This is when the plant contains the highest percentage of nitrogen. Rye is *alleopathic,* which means it bullies some other plants. Used as a cover crop, the victims are weeds. Dead or alive, it temporarily releases natural weed-suppressing chemicals into the soil. Try it in an area that has many weeds and let her rip.

SOYBEANS Easy-to-grow legume; fixes nitrogen and suppresses weeds. Long-season varieties make the largest plants. (These will not be the best tasting, but you're not after taste here: We're all about fixing the soil.)

VETCH, HAIRY Annual legume that grows well almost anywhere in the United States; requires adequate moisture and good soil. Plant in spring in northern climates and in fall in the South. Charming purple pea-like flowers attract beneficials, while the plant fixes nitrogen and loosens topsoil.

DIRT DIVA TIP
Some Legume Seeds Are Inoculated with a Bacterium

Rhizobium is a common soil bacterium and is safe to humans, plants, and animals. Inoculating the seeds helps ensure that you will have fancy nodules on your legumes that are filled with nitrogen. These hardworking nodules will be found around the roots, and you'll see them once you dig in the plant at the end of the season. Nodules are good. Ask your nursery person if the seeds have been inoculated. This may sound complicated, but I swear it's not. You can purchase a powder for inoculation for about a buck. Ask your seed supplier to give you the correct inoculant, if necessary.

A Plant Recommendation from the
Dirt Diva Royal Horticultural Society

Lathyrus odoratus
COMMON NAME: sweet pea

This nostalgic, romantic plant from the legume family has sweet-scented, butterfly-shaped flowers that come in crimson, pink, blue, white, and scarlet. This annual, fast-growing vine can reach up to 6 feet. Easily sown from seed outdoors after last frost date. In warmer climates, a second sowing is possible in the early fall for winter bloom. Sweet peas make beautiful cut flowers for a bouquet. This is both a nectar plant and a larval source for the gray hairstreak butterfly.

ORIGIN: Italy
HARDINESS: Zones 1–10
GROWING REQUIREMENTS: Loose, rich, well-drained soil. Needs sun to part sun and moderate water. Will bloom in spring and summer but doesn't like weather that's too hot or dry. Plant it near a fence or trellis.

THE UNIVERSAL BOTANICAL
WHAAA-WHAA RATING: **3**

21

Grow Your Own

Edible landscaping is as old as gardening itself, but with the recent food scares and the rapidly growing demand and popularity of organic and locally grown produce, it's back in the spotlight where it belongs. Instead of focusing on only ornamental plants in your yard, edible landscaping uses food-producing plants in the garden design as well. Here fruit trees, edible flowers, herbs, and ornamental plants are all combined.

Many modern-day home gardens were designed to have a vegetable garden in one area, cut flowers in another, and a rose garden off on its own in another section of the yard. That thinking is now becoming outdated. Monoculture is so 20 minutes ago! In today's sustainable garden design, edibles and ornamentals are best friends again! You can still have a raised bed full of organic greens and tomatoes, maybe near your kitchen, but you could also intermingle flowers and herbs that deter pests and invite pollinators and beneficial bugs to come visit.

WHY LANDSCAPE WITH EDIBLES?

- To enjoy the freshness and flavor of home-grown, fully ripened fruits and vegetables.
- To eliminate pesticides and herbicides used on the commercially grown foods you consume.
- To increase the food security of your household.
- To grow unusual varieties not available in stores.
- To get those kids away from computer and TV screens and outside appreciating the land that feeds them.

Planting

STEP 1: KNOW YOUR SOIL

Before planting vegetables, it's wise to do a soil test. Most vegetables thrive in soil with a pH between 6.0 and 6.8. In high rainfall areas you may need to add limestone (calcium) to raise the pH. In the arid west, you may need to add sulfur to lower the pH. Your local nursery will have a soil test kit and the necessary products to adjust your soil. If you live near the road, in the city, or in an old house and you have young children, you may also want to do a test for lead before growing edibles. Paint from old houses or car exhaust in an urban or roadside garden can linger in the soil for a long time. If you do find lead contamination, you may want to build a raised bed: lay out a thick mesh barrier cloth (sold at most nurseries) on the old soil, bring in fresh soil, and grow edibles in just that area.

STEP 2: FOLLOW THE SUN

Most leafy vegetables require 4 hours of direct sun a day and 6 to 8 hours if they bear fruit, so that should help you narrow down the best spot. If you have sun in only one section of your yard for that long of a period and the rest of the area is in the shade, feel free to make that your vegetable garden and forget about spreading edibles out across your entire landscape. You may even want to build a raised bed in that sunny spot. Raised beds in gardening are similar to using bowling bumpers in bowling; both make the game easier on you so you feel like a winner (or an 8-year-old, depending on how you look at it). Raised beds are usually a few degrees warmer than the level ground

HOW TO BUILD A RAISED BED

Choose a site with sun and good drainage. Then measure the area of your plot and sketch a rough plan on paper. Dig out weeds and level the area. Mark the bed with sticks and string. If gophers are a problem in your yard, put down a double layer of chicken wire. (This is probably a good idea even if you haven't had to deal with gopher-rage yet.) Next, build it up with fresh soil along with ¼ part well-rotted manure or compost to your desired height and length. Mix up the ingredients to a mound, shaping it into a bottomless, unframed bed with sloping sides. Then choose your frame; untreated wood, brick, stones, or concrete blocks. (Some woods are treated with arsenic to detract termites, so make sure to purchase untreated lumber. Let the lumberyard salesperson know you're going to be growing edibles, and he or she can advise you on your options.) Many garden stores are now offering snap-on pieces made of a variety of materials to frame a raised bed.

You may want to try growing the "Three Sisters": beans, corn, and squash, together in your raised bed. "The corn serves as a pole for your beans to climb. Beans, like other legumes, have bacteria living on their roots that help them absorb nitrogen from the air and convert it to a form that plants can use," says "the Garden Girl" Patti Moreno, editor at www .urbansustainableliving.com. "Corn requires a lot of nitrogen. The squash provides a layer of shade at soil level, keeping the weeds down and the moisture up."

and vegetables love warmth. The soil in a bed is deeper, looser, and less compacted, since it's never walked on. A raised bed will also improve a garden's appearance and accessibility.

STEP 3: KEEP DYSFUNCTIONAL RELATIVES APART

Start by drawing your design on a piece of graph paper and save this paper somewhere safe (not in the back of your messy desk drawer) for next year, so you can rotate your crops. Susceptibility to disease and pests runs in the family. You'll want to avoid planting members of the same plant family in the same spot next year. If you have the space, wait two to three years before bringing back family members. (For extra credit, try rotating your in-laws!) By rotating your crops each year, there's less chance of the same disease and the same pests coming in for an invasion on a certain botanical family. Another good idea is to grow cover crops in that same area every few seasons, so you're replenishing the soil after constantly using up its organic matter.

BOTANICAL FAMILIES OF COMMON VEGETABLE CROPS
Who's Your Daddy?

ONION *(ALLIACEAE)* Onion, leek, chive, garlic

SUNFLOWER *(ASTERACEAE)* Lettuce, endive, artichoke

CARROT *(APIACEAE)* Carrot, parsnip, parsley, celery

MUSTARD *(BRASSICACEAE)* Cabbage, kale, broccoli, Brussels sprouts, cauliflower, collards, kohlrabi, radish, turnip

GOOSEFOOT *(CHENOPODIACEAE)* Beet, spinach, chard

GOURD *(CUCURBITACEAE)* Cucumber, melon, squash, pumpkin, watermelon, gourd

PEA *(FABACEAE)* Legume, pea, bean, lima bean, soybean

NIGHTSHADE *(SOLANACEAE)* Pepper, tomato, potato, eggplant

STEP 4: KEEP BEST FRIENDS TOGETHER

Consider adding *companion plants* to your design. This practice combines folklore and modern-day research to help keep pests away from food crops. These are plants that seem to perform better with their best friend growing up right next to them. (Who wouldn't?) This happy coexistence is achieved by placing certain plants that actually ward off or confuse insect attacks next to your main crop. Many herbs fall into this category because of their powerful aroma. Other types of companion crops will attract beneficial insects. Some others are considered *attractant plants*, which will attract the pests, so they leave your main crop alone.

SOME WINNING COMPANION PLANTING COMBINATIONS

- Beautiful borage with its sweet blue star-shaped flowers is a fine companion for tomatoes, squash, and strawberries.
- Garlic planted near roses and raspberries can deter the persistent Japanese beetle from inviting all of his slacker friends to hang out.
- Marigolds are considered the workhorse of the companion plants and could be planted throughout the garden. Not only do they repel pests with their disturbing aroma, but some fastidious and harmful flying insects don't care for the gaudy shade of orange.
- Tansy planted under fruit trees and roses can deter flying insects, striped cucumber beetles, squash bugs, and ants.
- Nasturtium is best friends with radishes and cabbage and also hangs in the fruit tree clique. It is an attractant plant to aphids. Once the nasturtium is infested, throw out the plant and sow more seeds directly into the soil.
- Rosemary, one of the easiest and most eager herbs to grow, hangs with cabbage, beans, and carrots and can help deter cabbage moth, bean beetles, and carrot fly.

STEP 5: PLAN YOUR PLANTING

Most avid gardeners amend their vegetable plot in the *fall* to get it ready for spring. This is usually done by planting cover crops (see previous chapter) throughout the winter or by sheet mulching: composting with layers. To sheet mulch, weed the section you're going to use or mow it down. Cover the area with 2 inches of compost. Next, lay four layers of newspaper on top (black and white only). You could also use one layer of cardboard instead. Water it all well. Then cover it all up with 3 to 6 inches of straw or wood chips. This will kill the weeds and grass and rile up the earthworms to get busy tilling! By spring, organic matter will be decomposed and ready for you to start planting. (If you're super-serious about having nutritious soil, you could even poke holes in the sheet-mulched materials and plant

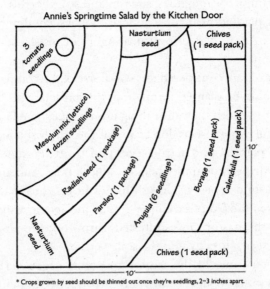

Annie's Springtime Salad by the Kitchen Door

3 tomato seedlings

Nasturtium seed

Chives (1 seed pack)

Mesclun mix (lettuce) 1 dozen seedlings

Radish seed (1 package)

Parsley (1 package)

Arugula (6 seedlings)

Borage (1 seed pack)

Calendula (1 seed pack)

10'

Nasturtium seed

Chives (1 seed pack)

10'

* Crops grown by seed should be thinned out once they're seedlings, 2–3 inches apart.

Hotness Note: In hot summer weather, replace lettuces (which can't stand the heat) with cucumbers or peppers or herbs such as basil or thyme.

some cover crop seeds in there. Oh, you will have earned my utmost respect and a gold star and a new pony!)

If you're reading this in the spring and you're just bursting at the seams to plant something edible, at least add plenty of compost before you plant any crops. Most fruits and vegetables (except tomatoes) are not deep rooters so you can mix compost in to only the top few inches or so. Vegetables and fruits can be tricky to grow and are extremely prone to a host of diseases and insect attacks. This could lead you to drink, smoke, swear, throw things, and plain ol' quit. Getting nutrients and water to the roots is critical for success. Starting off with healthy, well-amended soil will give you a better chance at beating the evildoer insects and diseases before they ruin your food and make you seem like a failure of a farmer.

Snacking and Drinking on the Job

If you're a novice gardener or an impatient one like yours truly, it's probably best to grow your vegetables from seedlings and not from seed. You should be safe to plant them in your garden after the last spring frost. Here in northern California, that's sometime in March. In cooler climates, it will be more like May. Once your seedlings are planted, you'll want to fertilize them once a month with an organic fertilizer if they are in pots. If they're in the ground and you added adequate compost or manure, they may be doing fine without extra feeding. However, if they seem like they're just sitting there quite comatose, like bumps on a log, you could side-dress each plant (feed around the drip line) once or twice during the growing season. For leafy crops such as lettuce, spinach, and Swiss chard, a nitrate-rich organic fertilizer (10-5-5) will boost foliar development. For beans, peas, squash, cucumber, pepper, and eggplant, a phosphorus-rich fertilizer (5-10-5) is best. Root crops such as radishes, turnips, beets, and carrots do well in a mixed fertilizer high in phosphorus and potassium (5-10-10). A homemade version would be to side-dress crops with a handful of compost, or a cup of aged manure, or 2 table-spoons alfalfa meal.

Keep an eye out for slugs and snails, who love to eat young seedlings. Pick them off and squish them into the ground. They're good compost and will be dinner to other wildlife hanging out in your yard searching for free food.

Most vegetables need 1 inch of water per week, except for toma-toes, which are rooted much deeper and are heavy drinkers. A drip system works best, although a winding soaker hose could suffice. Don't water vegetables with an overhead sprinkler. What, are ya crazy? That's inviting all the fungi in the entire neighborhood to your yard.

Last, in many climates, you can also plant cool-season crops in the fall and straight through the winter. Check with your local nurseries to see what they have in stock seasonally. If you're going to plant winter crops, be vigilant. Don't neglect them. When you hear of frost, cover them at night with a staked-up old sheet and remove it in the morning. If you are thinking, "Oy, shpilkes. Enough with the shmatas! Why does she make us work so hard just to grow a leaf of spinach?" don't grow cool-season crops.

DON'T BE A CHUMP WARNING

If watering by hand in containers, in hot weather, check on your crops twice a day. If they're drooping, water them slowly. Wildly soaking a drought-stressed crop could split its sides or make it sick, and then you'll blame me, and send me hate mail. (Send only if it's wrapped in English rose petals.)

For More Detailed Information on Specific Crops

Edible Landscaping, by Rosalind Creasy (Sierra Club, 2010)

Rodale's Vegetable Garden Problem Solver, by Fern Marshall Bradley (Rodale, 2007)

Fresh Food from Small Places, by R. J. Ruppenthal (Chelsea Green, 2008)

Pelargonium
COMMON NAME: scented geranium

Almond, apple, lime, nutmeg, peppermint, and rose are some of the scents of the highly fragrant leaves on scented geranium plants. Rose-scented geraniums are edible and are often found on pastries or as a salad garnish. These perennials will grow 1 to 3 feet tall and wide and are fantastic for herb gardens, window boxes, and hanging baskets. Peppermint geranium (*P. tomentosum*) even makes a good ground cover. Tiny pink or white flowers will bloom in the spring, but the main event is the heavenly fragrance of the fuzzy leaves when brushed against. Rose-scented (*P. graveolens*) is one of my favorites.

ORIGIN: South Africa
HARDINESS: Zones 7–11
GROWING REQUIREMENTS: Full sun, though peppermint geranium will grow in shade. Well-amended soil and low water. Deadhead regularly. Easy to propagate by cuttings. I've had no pest or disease problems with these scented sensations. Go get some! Buy the small size. They're fast growers.

THE UNIVERSAL BOTANICAL
WHAAA–WHAA RATING: **1**

22
Herb Gardens

Herbs are the perfect starter plants for novice gardeners because they truly are undemanding plants. Because of the substances that create their aromas, they're rarely bothered by pests yet they attract beneficial bugs and pollinating bees. Diseases are also rare. Although they will perform their best in a sunny area with well-drained soil, most herbs are so easygoing that they can adapt to dry or less-fertile soil. Perennial herbs make a good framework for an ornamental garden, while annual herbs such as basil and dill can be used to fill in spare spaces among perennial herbs or other garden plants. Annual herbs will grow for just one season, so you'll need to plant anew each spring. Some common annuals are anise, basil, German chamomile, cilantro, and dill; common perennials are bee balm, catnip, chives, lavender, lemon balm, lovage, lemongrass, marjoram, mint, oregano, rosemary, sage, tarragon, and thyme. There are a few herbs that will survive in light shade or shade. Angelica, chervil, ginseng, lungwort, sweet woodruff, tarragon, comfrey, and elderberry can be planted in areas receiving less sunlight.

Herb Dealings

When purchasing herbs at the nursery, buy the seedlings in 2- or 4-inch containers instead of growing each herb from seed. You'll want only one or two of a certain type of herb, so you won't need a whole pack of seeds. Plus, many herbs grow very slowly from seed, making us sigh and doubt. Do we need that? No. Buy the seedlings, rub the leaves for the calming aroma, and get on with it.

Top-dress the soil with compost and plant herbs. Plant some near the kitchen but also spread them around the garden. They're beautiful, low-maintenance, and low-water plants to grow. Some herbs can be propagated by cuttings. This can be done in the spring or late summer. This will allow plants to put out strong roots by winter. Some of the easiest herbs for cuttings are basil, bee balm, lemon verbena, mints, rosemary, salvias, scented geraniums, and artemisia. (See Chapter 19 for how to make a cutting.)

CONTAINERS

Herbs make terrific container plants. Make sure the pots have good drainage and fresh potting mix each year. Herbs can also be placed in small pots or in a window box on a windowsill. In an 18-inch window box you can easily plant four to six starter herbs. Be sure to water a few times a week in the summer heat, since the roots have little insulating soil to protect them from the summer sun. Basil, bay, chives, dill, parsley, sage, thyme, and lemon verbena can be grown indoors as long as they receive as much light as possible, maybe near a south-facing window.

CARE

Most herbs will thrive without fertilizer and are sensitive to overfeeding. Instead add a natural fertilizer in the spring when you first plant,

FIVE EASY HERBS TO GROW

Basil This is a tender annual used in cooking. There are now many varieties such as lemon, cinnamon, and cloves.

Fennel This is a perennial or a self-sowing annual herb that smells like licorice. The base can be eaten as a vegetable while the feathery foliage can be used as a garnish. Most varieties grow 3 to 5 feet tall. Plant away from many other plants, as fennel has two personalities and very few friends. The evil side adversely affects the growth of nearby plants, while the good side attracts beneficial bugs and butterflies to your garden with its clusters of small flowers.

Mint This is by far the easiest herb to grow and comes in flavors of orange, apple, lemon, and chocolate! They are notorious spreaders, so planting in containers is best. Can easily be divided to share with friends in small pots.

Pineapple Sage This is one of my all-time favorites. The leaves and red flowers are edible, and it attracts hummingbirds. It grows well in the ground or in a pot from late spring to early fall without making a fuss.

Thyme This is a low-growing aromatic perennial creeper with ornamental and culinary qualities. It flourishes in sandy, dry soil in full sun and comes in an array of varieties: lemon, lime, cinnamon, apple, orange, and nutmeg.

such as compost or alfalfa meal. If they're looking straggly or yellow midseason, a shot of liquid fish emulsion mixed in water should get them back in the game. If you're growing them for culinary purposes, you won't want to fertilize much, as this will give you large, lush plants. Instead you'll want the essential oils more concentrated. You'll also want to deadhead the flowers and focus on the tasty leaves.

Perennial herbs like lavender, rosemary, and many salvias would do well with an early springtime pruning to rejuvenate the plant. If you can stand the temporary crew cut, cut the plant back by half.

HARVESTING

Collect leaves for culinary and medicinal use before the plant begins flowering. Cut herbs in the morning because this is when the essential oils are most concentrated. Cut back just above a leaf so that you're encouraging a bushy growth on the remaining plant.

SOME SMART HERBAL COMPANION PLANTINGS

Though companion planting is a combination of folklore and fact, I believe it's worth a try.

Basil Good companion to tomatoes; repels flies and mosquitoes.

Borage Companion to tomatoes; deters tomato worm.

Dill Companion to cabbage; invites beneficial predatory wasps.

Garlic Plant near roses and raspberries; deters Japanese beetle and aphids.

Mint Companion to cabbage and tomatoes; deters white cabbage moth.

Rosemary Companion to cabbage, beans, and carrots; deters bean beetles and carrot fly.

Sage Companion to rosemary, cabbage, and carrots; deters cabbage moth and carrot fly.

Tansy Plant under fruit trees; deters flying insects, Japanese beetles, squash bugs, and ants.

Thyme Companion to cabbage, potatoes, and tomatoes; deters cabbage worm.

A Plant Recommendation from the
Dirt Diva Royal Horticultural Society

Lavandula angustifolia
COMMON NAME: English lavender

If you garden in a dry, Mediterranean climate, as I do, you will love growing lavender! Most species grow 2 to 3 feet high and wide with small mauve flowers in erect, short spikes on grayish green stems in late spring and summer. Many pests are repelled by lavender's strong scent. Lavenders attract bees and butterflies, both beneficial pollinators to your yard, and are also good indoor container plants for cooler climates, as long as you have them placed near a sunny window. English lavender is one of the most fragrant species and is often used in lavender herbal tinctures and soap. It's also one of the less floppy and more erect species of lavender. Good as a short hedge. The hybrid 'Grosso', also named 'Fat Spike', is possibly the most fragrant lavender of all.

ORIGIN: Mediterranean Region
HARDINESS: Zones 6–10
GROWING REQUIREMENTS: Lavenders prefer full sun and well-drained soil, thriving in both acid or alkaline soils. Most are moderately frost hardy and can be propagated from seed or cuttings in the summer. All species of lavender are noteworthy low-water and low-maintenance plants to have in your garden.

THE UNIVERSAL BOTANICAL
WHAAA–WHAA RATING: **1**

23
Return of the Killer Tomatoes

My twin sister, Carol, lives in sunny San Diego, probably the best climate zone to grow most crops, but claims she doesn't have time to garden. It's true, she's busy 24/7, multitasking as a doctor and the super-mom of two nearly perfect children. But every few years, seemingly out of the blue, she finds some spare time and *gets all giddy for gardening*. She has a sunny, though small area of fertile soil in her backyard where she and her daughters, almost upon an impulse, plant their vegetable garden. This is when she calls me for free horticultural advice, which I gladly give to her. It makes me feel all warm and fuzzy and sisterly and generous. But after I hang up, I always get a bad case of, "No way. Not this year. Not over my dead body-itis." Sibling rivalry is never a pretty thing. I imagine her growing better tomatoes than me, and then chirping and chiming to all her girlfriends how easy it is and that "any idiot can grow tomatoes." This doesn't sit well with me.

So, every summer I pull out my gargantuan, irrefutable plant encyclopedia and turn to the earmarked chapter, "How to Outperform Your Evil Twin Sister, Organically." And then I get to work. Here's the scoop on growing tomatoes:

Tomatoes are the favorite crop to grow in American home gardens. If you have a sunny and warm spot in your garden, preferably with southern exposure, you'll likely be successful. Before planting, turn your soil a bit and blend in plenty of compost. Tomato plants crave phosphorus and calcium, so you could add a handful of bonemeal at this time. If you have Epsom salts handy, sprinkle a teaspoon into each hole for magnesium, which promotes plant vitality and productivity. Tomatoes produce a harvest in 70 to 80 days, so be patient and be prepared to keep monitoring their growth, checking for problems that can arise from erratic weather to pests to fungus.

You have a choice to grow tomatoes from a package of seeds or a 4-inch seedling or a gallon container. All are fine options, depending on how patient you are! If you grow them by seed, you'll have a wide range of cultivars and heirloom varieties that you may not find at local garden centers. But you'll have to sow the seeds 2 months before planting outside. Wait till the last frost in your area has passed before planting your seedlings in the ground.

Once home-grown or store-bought seedlings are ready to plant, choose a cloudy day to place in the ground to lessen plant shock. Space tomato plants 1 to 2 feet apart if they will be trained up on a trellis or caged, in well-amended soil. This will give them good circulation while providing adequate room for caging or staking. If you're going to let the plant sprawl on the ground, space them 3 to 4 feet apart. Either way is fine. Pull off the bottom leaf or leaves of the seedling and bury half the plant's stem into the ground carefully without disturbing the roots any more than necessary. Allowing roots to form where the bottom leaves used to be makes for a stronger root system, and some growers say this produces higher yields.

Not sure if you should sprawl or stake your tomatoes? Letting plants sprawl requires less work and can have higher yields, but there's more chance of insects or disease coming around for a visit. I prefer caging my plants. You can buy inexpensive metal cages at your local nursery, which will last for years. These cages are 5- to 6-foot-tall circular galvanized fencing that you grow your tomatoes inside of whether planting in the ground or in a pot. Caging plants takes up less garden space, provides support for heavy tomato-laden branches, offers a little shade with its leaves protecting the plant from sun scald, and helps protect plants from decay and pests. Plus, it makes you look like you know what you're doing. In my playbook, that's half the job right there.

Another idea if your soil is jam-packed with fungal spores is to hang up your tomato plants and grow them upside down. I know that sounds ludicrous but it's actually brilliant. The upside-down planter is sturdy, provides continuous water without you watering it each day, is out of reach of most pests, and is much more resistant to soil-borne diseases. There's a container up at the top that you place water in every few days and it slowly waters the plant. You simply hang it in a sunny spot along with fresh, clean potting mix and compost, and stand back! Watch and learn. I can't say enough positive things about this revolutionary way to grow tomatoes only that I wish I had found it sooner.

Once planted, water well. If the nighttime temperatures are still below 50°F in your area when you first plant your seedlings in the ground, you may want to invest in the Wall O Water, which is widely available at plant centers. This is a plastic sheet of circular cones that you fill with water and place around the plant to absorb heat from the sun during the day and radiate it back to the plant at night. Tomatoes are subtropical plants that thrive in uniformly moderate temperatures of 65° to 85°F. If you have chilly nights, the leaves will start to turn yellow or pale green and the growth will be stunted. The really bad part is that plants struggling with cold night temperatures can be set back for weeks. Carefully and gently remove the Wall O Water in a month or so, when the day and nighttime temperatures begin to rise. This would be a good time to add a cage around the plant if you haven't yet, as plants will be larger and ready to spread their wings. At this time, place a thick layer of mulch around the plant to retain moisture. (Don't add mulch when first planting. At that critical time, tomatoes need direct heat.)

Pruning

If you stake or cage your tomatoes, you can prune them periodically throughout the growing season to produce higher yields and let in air and light, forcing them to ripen earlier. All you do is use your fingers to snap off suckers (small, skinny sprouts that grow in the fold of the main stem and the side stem). You can leave a few suckers on the top of the plant to protect from sun scald.

Note: Only prune "indeterminate" tomatoes; "determinate" ones need no pruning. It will usually say which type it is on the seed pack or nursery plant label. Determinate tomatoes all bear fruit around the same time and then kick the bucket, while indeterminate tomatoes keep growing foliage and fruit till they freeze to death in late fall.

Watering and Feeding

Tomatoes require deep and consistent watering all summer. If you can't commit to this, you may as well forget this venture. Underwatering, overwatering, and inconsistent watering will bring you to your knees when you see undersized or, worse yet, no fruit at all, or tomatoes with all sorts of physiological problems. So make sure when you water that you're reaching a couple feet down into the soil for established tomato plants and try to be consistent in your watering. Try to keep the leaves from getting wet and inviting fungal spores.

Don't call me with your knickers in a twist if you see the bottom leaves of your tomato plant turning yellow or brown about a month after planting. That's normal. It could mean the plant is lacking nitrogen if it gets worse. But don't add any fertilizer until the plant flowers. Once the first flowers form, side-dress with an organic fertilizer low in nitrogen (5-10-10) and do the same thing a month later. You can also use a quart of compost tea instead.

Growing Tomatoes in Containers

Tomatoes are perfect to grow on a sunny deck or balcony. You can grow full-size plants in large wooden barrels, 5-gallon containers, or fiberglass tubs. If you have less room, try growing dwarf cherry tomatoes. These can be grown in a 12-inch pot. (Some productive choices are 'Tiny Tim' and 'Pixie Hybrid II'.) Don't use soil from your garden. This is too dense and is probably filled with pests that would love to ruin your tomato-growing competition. Plant in a store-bought clean potting mix. Add a starter fertilizer rich in phosphorus like E. B. Stone's Sure Start or FoxFarm's Jump Start. Water frequently and feed every 2 weeks with compost tea or a (5-10-10) liquid fertilizer.

HARVESTING

Leave the fruit on the plant for at least 4 weeks after it swells into a fruit. This way they are deliciously ripe and will taste much better than if picked early. Do *not* store your tomatoes in the refrigerator. That's so 1950s! You may as well pull out the bowl of plastic fruit like your mom had on the coffee table, next to the couch covered with clear plastic that you weren't allowed to sit on. Refrigeration ruins one of Mother Nature's most universally loved homegrown tastes. For better taste, store them out of direct sunlight on a countertop (so you can show them off).

Tomatoes Have Issues Too! What's Bugging Them?

All crops have pest and disease issues, but tomatoes seem to have more than their fair share. If the growing conditions are not perfect, your tomato plants may look unhealthy and discourage you and your tomato-growing project midseason. Hang in there, soldier. Some diseases or problems are easy to correct by simply removing the infected branch. Oftentimes the rest of the plant will survive and the blemished fruit can still be eaten.

ALTERNARIA BLIGHT (EARLY BLIGHT) The leaves turn brown to black with dark spots developing into concentric rings in the shape of a target. Lower leaves are usually attacked first and may dry up and die. The same target spots may show up on branches, stems, and fruit. Dispose of heavily infected plants in the trash before it spreads to other tomato plants. Try a different variety to grow in a new location.

BLOSSOM-END ROT There's a hot, dry spell just when your tomatoes are starting to ripen and suddenly your tomatoes have large brown and black spots on them making them look like damaged goods. They may be toast! You'll know in another week or so. In the future, mulch and keep a watchful eye on them, especially when you hear about hot spells on the way. Try a different variety and make sure to add plenty of compost and bonemeal at planting time. Blossom-end rot can be caused by a shortage of calcium (which bonemeal will add) or by uneven watering. Don't let plants dry out.

NEMATODES Tiny worm-like creatures that attack a tomato plant's roots, stunting growth, wilting the plant, and lowering its disease resistance. Try soil solarization and crop rotation after this year's crop either survives or goes bust.

SUN SCALD This occurs when green or ripening tomatoes get too much sun. At first a white patch appears on the side of the tomato facing the sun. Then it grows bigger and turns gray. You can leave them on the plant and cut off the nasty part when they're ripe. Prune tomato plants less, so the top leaves can help shade the fruit in extremely sunny and dry conditions.

LEAF SPOT This is a bad fungal disease that occurs where there's warm and moist summer weather. Leaves turn yellow and drop off. Sadly, the fungus lives in old tomato vines, in the soil, and on perennial weeds. Rotating crops may help next summer, or plant tomatoes in fresh clean potting mix in 5-gallon containers.

FUSARIUM AND VERTICILLIUM WILT These two fungal wilts attack many flowers and vegetables but are especially fond of tomatoes. Like an uninvited, irritating, ungrateful house guest, these wilts will stays in your soil for years. The first symptom is the wilting of older leaves, followed by yellowing leaves and brown V-shaped patterns on the leaves. The plant will stop growing even with proper watering and feeding. (Ouch, stop throwing things at me! I'm just the messenger.) Don't feel bad. Here in the Bay Area, with the combination of fog and then extremely dry weather, it's very common for us to have infected soil. I have this in my garden, so, each spring, I plant my tomato seedlings in fresh potting mix in 5-gallon plastic containers or in a hanging upside-down planter. I make sure to keep the pots away from any infected flower boxes because most of these evil stalker-spores survive travel through soil, air, and water.

TOBACCO MOSAIC VIRUS Don't let smokers touch your tomato plants. They'll spread the disease. Nicotine is present in some plants and is toxic (surprise!) to soft-bodied insects and humans. Symptoms are stunted, dying, pale-colored leaves and brown-spotted fruit. The virus will linger only for that season in your soil and then it will go invade some poor smoker's yard.

After reading about all that could go wrong growing tomatoes, don't you have greater admiration for the farmers who grow our food? If you find you're using up too much water each summer, while also fighting off pests and diseases, and you're still not producing healthy tomatoes, do what my friend Charlie, an extraordinary gardener in fruitful Santa Cruz, California, did. He stopped growing them. Instead he buys them at his local farmers market. This way you're supporting the farmer instead of feeling defeated, puny, frustrated, and enraged. That's not gardening. Save that for the office!

Breaking the Code on Disease-Resistant Varieties

I make sure to only purchase seedlings that are resistant to a few of the worst tomato diseases out there. Look for these letters V, F, N, T, and A on the plant labels when purchasing. This is how the tag will read:

Resistant to: V = Verticillium Wilt, F = Fusarium Wilt, N = Nematode, T = Tobacco Mosaic Virus, A= Alternaria blight.

Resistance to these problems doesn't mean they're completely immune. Good cultural and nurturing practices are still important. Though it's no guarantee your tomatoes won't get infected, you've at least given yourself a chance of tasting the fruits of your labor.

Last, be a Secret Agent: Infiltrate your neighborhood and see who has the healthiest-looking tomatoes growing right there in your microclimate. Act like a normal person with a generous nature and kindly ask them which kind of tomatoes they grew. Copy them and take all the credit.

A PLANT RECOMMENDATION FROM THE
DIRT DIVA ROYAL HORTICULTURAL SOCIETY

Salvia spathacea
COMMON NAME: hummingbird or pitcher sage

Most salvias will attract hummingbirds, butterflies, bees, and insect allies to come eat the pests off of your summer vegetable garden. Pitcher sage requires little water and makes elegant cut flowers. It has sticky aromatic leaves and can grow 3 to 5 feet tall. Unusual magenta ball-like blossoms bloom in spirals of tightly packed clusters in the late spring. This is an easy plant to grow and when in bloom, a real show-stealer.

ORIGIN: California native
HARDINESS: Zones 7–10
GROWING REQUIREMENTS: Most salvias are sun worshipers, but in very hot areas, light shade may be fine. Give them a bit of compost when planting and then little water, and they'll be content. Drought tolerant and deer resistant.

THE UNIVERSAL BOTANICAL
WHAAA-WHAA RATING: **3**

24

Flowers Good
Enuf to Eat

Cooking with flowers is an ancient tradition that has been traced back to Roman times. Flowers from the garden, notably roses and orange blossoms, were used both ornamentally and for culinary purposes during the Victorian era. Cookbooks during that time contain recipes for salads and soups flavored by violets, marigolds, primroses, lavender, rose hips, and strawberry leaves, among others. Today edible flowers are a popular way to show off and impress your friends. C'mon, you know you want to. But first, a few safety guidelines.

Safety Guidelines

Use only those flowers you *know* are edible. If you have any questions, call your local poison control center. Never, ever eat flowers bought from the florist. Why? The flowers most likely have been sprayed with pesticides that have been manufactured in the United States but are outlawed to use here because they've been found to be carcinogenic.

So, instead, these chemicals are sent to foreign countries that have less stringent pesticide regulation, to be sprayed on flowers and food by farmers there. Then those bouquets and crops are shipped back to the States to sell at our florists and supermarkets. In the biz, we refer to this as "the circle of poison." Sounds like someone was drunk on Methoxychlor with a twist of Endosulfan sulfate and got the whole idea of "recycle, reduce, and reuse" all wrong, doesn't it?

Don't eat flowers growing by the roadside or in dark alleys. (Have you lost your mind?) Be sure to use only organically grown flowers from your own yard. Use ones you know are edible and haven't been sprayed with any garden products at all, even organic ones. Also, if you're new to edible flowers or you have hay fever or asthma, consume only a small bit to make sure you're not allergic to the plant.

Harvest

Harvest flowers in the morning if possible. Wash them quickly in cool water, shake them out, and dry them on a paper towel. Examine them carefully again to make sure there aren't any tiny insects hiding in between the petals. If you won't be eating them right away, store them between damp layers of paper towels in the refrigerator. Before using them, rinse and check again for insects.

EDIBLE FLOWERS THAT ARE WIDELY RECOGNIZED AS SAFE TO INGEST

NASTURTIUM *(TROPAEOLUM MAJUS)* We are fortunate that nasturtiums grow around our yard almost as invasive as a weed. Luckily we love nasturtiums and use them in salads, sandwiches, omelets, and soups. Nasturtium's round-shaped leaves and the brilliant sunset-colored blossoms on the vine are both edible and have a peppery taste similar to watercress. Nasturtiums grow best in poor soil and can stand some neglect, so this is a great flower to grow for novice gardeners or children, or my sister Sharon, Queen of the Plastic Houseplant. Nasturtiums are annuals and grow best in full sun. There are a variety of cultivars that all grow easily from seed: dwarf, tall, or climbing from 1 to 3 feet.

BORAGE *(BORAGO OFFICINALIS)* I planted a few borage seeds about 3 years ago and now every spring we have large areas of borage spreading almost like a ground cover around the yard. The delicate star-shaped flowers on the borage plant are a beautiful, hypnotizing clear blue. The blossoms are sweet and small, similar to a forget-me-not (*Myosotis*) and have a cool cucumber taste. Borage blossoms can be used to garnish lemonade, sorbet, or a gin and tonic! In the summer, kids enjoy freezing them in an ice tray. The leaves are also good in a salad, but need to be chopped finely to reduce the furry texture. Borage can easily be grown by seed. Plants do best in full sun but can stand light shade. Borage will self-sow for years to come.

CALENDULA OR POT MARIGOLD *(CALENDULA OFFICINALIS)* Calendula was used in medieval times to effectively treat a variety of ailments. During the Renaissance, calendulas were prescribed for toothaches. The yellow or orange petals can easily be plucked from the flower head. A fresh handful of Calendula petals look lovely tossed onto a salad of mixed greens. Dried petals can be stirred into chowders, muffin mixes, or paella, as a homegrown sharp substitute for saffron. Calendula grows to 18 inches and does best in full sun. Calendulas look best in the early summer and then get a bit straggly during the hotter days of August. Cut back after first bloom to encourage new growth. These are one of the easiest annuals to grow from seed. They're low maintenance, generous, dependable annuals and will happily self-sow.

LEEKS, CHIVES, GARLIC *(ALLIUM)* Known as the "flowering onions," there are approximately 400 species, including onions, garlic, chives, and shallots. All members of this genus are edible, and all parts of the plant are edible. The flowers are commonly lavender-pink and have a stronger flavor than the leaves. The leaves and flowers can be added to a salad. Break apart the florets and add them to cooked vegetables, egg dishes, potatoes, and cream cheese. The leaves can also be cooked in soups and stews. Seeds, bulbs, or nursery plants can be planted in mild winter climates in autumn in rich, well-drained soil in a sunny location.

SCENTED GERANIUM *(PELARGONIUM GRAVEOLENS)* Scented geranium is a simple, low-maintenance perennial. The leaves are rose scented (there are other flavors too, such as peppermint and ginger) and bloom profusely with tiny pink flowers in the spring. Wedding cake designers like my pal Genevieve Haag, aka Sister Sledge, will line a cake pan with whole flowers to scent one of her spectacular wedding cakes. Or she'll use the petals on the top as garnish. Finally . . . a good reason to get married!

JOHNNY-JUMP-UP *(VIOLA TRICOLOR)* This annual blooms profusely with little care in sun or shade, and self-sows with small yellow, white, and purple flowers. They bloom best in cool weather and have a slight wintergreen flavor. They make a pretty decoration for salads and dessert, or simply float the flower in a punchbowl.

CHAMOMILE *(MATRICARIA RECUTITA)* This 2- to 3-foot-tall annual has finely cut foliage with minute daisy-like flowers. The leaves and flowers have a light apple fragrance and make a popular tea. Chamomile grows well in full sun to part shade and once established will reseed. To make a cup of chamomile tea, harvest the flowers when their petals begin to droop. Place 3 teaspoons of fresh flowers in a cup of boiling water. Cover and steep for 3 minutes. Avoid chamomile if you're sensitive to ragweed.

LAVENDER *(LAVANDULA ANGUSTIFOLIA)* This fragrant flower brings to mind purity, tranquility, and relaxation. Its fresh clean scent was the favorite bath-water additive throughout Greek and Roman history. It was popular not only for its long-lasting fragrance but for its insect-repelling properties. The purple flowers can be used to flavor jams or to make lavender vinegar. They can also be mixed in with savory herbs for fragrant stews. The flower can also be used in a tea to calm the nerves. Easy to grow in a dry and sunny location.

BEE BALM *(MONARDA DIDYMA)* This beautiful perennial sparkles in the summer with shaggy heads of tight tubular scarlet, pink, or purple blossoms. It can be grown in sun or part shade, grows to about 3 feet tall, and invites many pollinators to your yard. The flowers can be used to scatter on salads, as garnishes, or to make bee balm tea. Bee balm flowers have a citrus and minty flavor.

ROSE *(ROSA)* Rose petals can be added to meat dishes, fruit salads, and desserts. Choose roses with the strongest scent to have the most flavor. Make sure you choose from rosebushes that have not been sprayed with any chemicals. Polyantha roses and/or rosebushes with shiny, dark green leaves are usually safer and less prone to rose diseases.

DON'T BE A CHUMP WARNING

Here are a few common poisonous flowers. **Don't eat them!** You want a knuckle sandwich? Azalea, calla lily, crocus, daffodil, delphinium, foxglove, hyacinth, hydrangea, iris, lantana, larkspur, lobelia, lupine, oleander, poinsettia, ranunculus, rhododendron, sweet pea, wisteria, and the leaves of tomatoes, potatoes, peppers, and eggplant.

Some other edible flowers are chives, coriander, dill, fennel, garlic, rosemary, and pineapple sage.

A few mail-order seed catalogs with plenty of edible flower choices are Johnny's Selected Seeds, The Gourmet Gardener, Shepherd's Garden Seeds, Thompson & Morgan, and Renee's Garden Seeds.

A Plant Recommendation from the
Dirt Diva Royal Horticultural Society

Monarda

COMMON NAME: bee balm, bergamot

Bee balm flower heads are unique: pink, magenta, or red clusters of tubular flowers beckon to you on tall spires in midsummer. Bergamot (*M. fistulosa*) foliage has a lemony fragrance and is used in teas. The flowers make an edible garnish to salads and are a great source of pollen and nectar for butterflies, bees, and hummingbirds. *M. didyma* (bee balm) is probably the most common and is one of the showiest. 'Aquarius' has deep purple flowers, while the hybrid 'Mahogany' has wine red or lilac flowers. Most species are frost hardy.

ORIGIN: United States

HARDINESS: Zones 4–10

GROWING REQUIREMENTS: Grow in moderately moist soil in full sun or dappled shade. Moderate watering.

THE UNIVERSAL BOTANICAL
WHAAA-WHAA RATING: **5**

25
Fruit Tree Helper

There's a misconception about growing fruit trees. Novice garden-ers think they're hard to grow and can be achieved only by expe-rienced gardeners. We just want you to think that way to make us feel better about ourselves. . . . Fruit trees are actually easy to grow if you have loads of sun and if you're patient. There's that dreadful P-word again. Bah! It may take a few seasons till you get a tree full of fruit, but once you do, you'll have free fruit for years to come.

When choosing which fruit tree to plant, decide if you have enough room for a standard fruit tree, which can grow to 30 or 40 feet tall. You may want to go with dwarf trees, which grow between 10 and 20 feet when mature. Choosing disease-resistant trees is also a wise idea. You'll worry less about keeping your trees healthy and free of pests. You'll also want to consider your local climate. Fruit trees require a certain amount of hours in either a low-chill period or a high-chill period to break dormancy and develop fruit properly. You can find this information at your local garden nursery or at your local Master Gardener office, where they often have a list of the easiest and most disease-resistant fruit trees in your climate zone. They can also help you find a fruit tree that is self-pollinating so that a second compatible cultivar planted nearby isn't necessary. Many peaches, nectarines, and tart cherries are self-fruitful as well as some apples, pears, and European plums. Make sure to plant your new tree where deer can't come for their early bird special. Plant them in mixed borders or near the vegetable garden or in a large pot on a patio, as long as there's full sun in those areas. Even 1 or 2 hours of daily shade can make fruit smaller and less colorful.

Planting

Depending on where you live, you can plant a new fruit tree in the fall or spring. Check with your local nursery. Once you've chosen your tree, make sure the area where you plant has good drainage and is in full sun. Fruit trees perform best in soil high in calcium, magnesium, and potassium, while too much nitrogen can lead to lush foliar growth, inviting pests and disease instead of fruit, so a soil test is a good idea.

We all want to toss a bunch of compost and fertilizer into the hole we're digging for a new fruit tree, but recent studies have shown this can actually hinder the tree. According to my bible, *Rodale's Ultimate Encyclopedia of Organic Gardening*, it makes the tree just want to sit right where it is (on the couch) instead of spreading its roots any farther. This makes trees susceptible to toppling over in high winds. It also makes them prone to wilting in drought and makes the amended roots too wet during rainy periods. Instead, lightly rake in a top layer of compost in the area where you'll be planting. Amend the area out to where you think the full-grown tree's leaf canopy will reach. Plant the tree. See Chapter 11 for full instructions on how to plant a tree. Some gardeners like to dip the young tree's roots in powdered bonemeal to help it along. Others apply compost tea at planting.

Once planted, soak the roots deeply once a week with a hose for the first year. Moisture is critical to the young roots. After the first year of weekly deep watering, regularly check to see if the tree needs watering by dipping a finger into the soil 3 inches down. If the soil is dry at 3 inches down, the tree needs a good soaking. Aim to get water down a few feet.

Fertilizing

If you are adding compost to your yard once or twice a year, you probably won't need to fertilize your fruit trees at all. Monitor your tree and see that it's growing close to a foot a year. If your tree is lagging in fruit production, fertilize in the spring only with a thick layer of compost. Many organic farmers spray their fruit trees with a foliar seaweed or kelp spray when buds start to show color. These sprays are available at nurseries or online. Foliar sprays are said to be absorbed by the plants 20 times faster than adding fertilizer to the roots. Here the tree's leaves take in the nutrients through their stomata, tiny pores in the leaves.

Pests and Disease

You may have heard the term *dormant spraying*. Dormant spraying is a heedful option if you've had challenging pest infestations on your fruit trees in the past. Some pests come for the winter holidays and want to hang out, suck vital plant nutrients from your fruit trees, lay eggs, and never leave. Many dormant spray oils will smother or create mild disruptions to the pests' diet or surroundings. However, don't feel that you must spray your fruit trees just because your neighbors do. If you haven't been using any synthetic pesticides or man-made neon blue plant fertilizer in your yard, there's a good chance you still have insect allies coming for a visit to take these overwintering insects and eggs off your hands without you interfering.

Peach leaf curl is a common water-activated fungus that is hard to stop once it starts on stone fruit trees. Lime sulfur or copper sulfate sprays will help prevent and control it, as well as scab and powdery mildew. Nell Newman, cofounder of Newman's Own Organics, organic gardener, and author of *The Newman's Own Organics: Guide to a Good Life*, shares these tips:

> First and foremost, plant varieties of peaches which are resistant to peach leaf curl. A few varieties are Red Haven, Avalon Pride, and Frost. Check with your local nursery for recommendations or, if there is a peach grower at your local farmers market, you can ask them. At the first sign of curl, remove and destroy all the diseased leaves and keep the ground free of dropped leaves or fruit. Kelp spray is a good foliar feed once a month during the summer, and Neem oil helps to control the spread of various diseases. There are many substitutes now for the old blood and bonemeal approach, such as mineral greensand for potassium, kelp meal for potash, and soft rock for phosphorus. Finally, lime sulfur keeps the disease in check if sprayed when the leaves drop.

If you do choose to spray, always spray *after* the tree has lost all of its leaves. (On the West Coast this can be early winter, but it could be late winter on the East Coast.) Three applications are best. Here in California, we aim for easy dates to remember like Thanksgiving, New Year's Day, and Valentine's Day. Once the tree is stripped, any insects and/or disease is exposed, so this is good time to apply a horticultural oil, lime sulfur, or a copper sulfate fungicide, which can be found at your local nursery. Make sure to water the tree well before spraying and don't spray on rainy or windy days. For best results, thoroughly coat the branches, twigs, and fallen leaves. It's also a good idea to clean up fallen leaves before and after spraying and then cover the area with clean mulch. You'll want to choose products that have very low toxicity to people and animals. However, anything that kills insects may have other side effects so wear protective clothing, gloves, and goggles. Always read the label and follow the directions exactly. Just because these products are organic or natural doesn't mean they're completely harmless. (When you're done with this project, take off your spraying outfit and toss it into the wash.)

There's an extensive list of less toxic product options at Our Water—Our World (www.ourwaterourworld.org). If you're going to try these, or other mixtures, make sure you purchase them at a plant nursery not a chain store's garden section where the gardening staff isn't trained in integrated pest management (IPM). If possible, first contact your local Master Gardeners at your County Cooperative Extension to make sure you're correctly diagnosing the problem. Some of these products used at the wrong time or on the wrong tree can cause damage.

Fruit Tree Pruning Advice

First, I recommend you get yourself a good book on the art of proper fruit tree pruning, since a poorly pruned fruit tree can seriously jeopardize its fruit production. And each type of fruit tree has its very own neuroses, peevishness, and idiosyncrasies.

The Backyard Orchardist by Stella Otto is a handbook that many Master Gardeners recommend. Having a visual reference to go by can be a good thing, and I don't want to be blamed for your lopsided, dipstick tree that failed to produce fruit. I've got enough horticultural baggage of my own, thank you. Also, if leaves or buds have appeared on your fruit trees already in the winter, dormancy is over and it's too late to prune. Better luck next year, Slacker.

Pruning your fruit trees in the late winter stimulates growth and increases fruiting while also opening the interior of a tree to sunlight. Having pruned my rosebushes right after New Year's, I like to prune my fruit trees the day after Valentine's Day. Depending on what Bill, my sweetheart of 20 years, has given me the day before, that sets up my emotional radar, and only then do I decide if this year's fruit tree trimming will be a light and delicate affair or a ruthless slice-and-dice fest.

If you want fruit, you need loads of sunshine! Sometimes you'll see fruit only on the top, exterior branches of the tree because that's where the most direct sunlight shines. Thinning out and opening up the tree to light will ripen fruit, improve air circulation, discourage disease, and let birds swoop in to eat preying insects. But don't go overboard; too much pruning can stimulate growth but reduce fruiting, so it's better to prune lightly. Apples, cherries, figs, and citrus trees require minimal pruning, while most stone fruit (peaches, plums, nectarines) require more extensive pruning and may need to be pruned in the spring instead of the late winter in colder climates. Once again, it's best to check with your local nursery or Master Gardeners.

After the summer/fall harvest, pick up all fruit that falls to the ground and toss it into your compost pile. This way you won't be inviting pests or fungal spores to your yard. Have a fruit-tossing competition. That's what I do with my son, Jack. We see who can throw the farthest. It's the only way, besides cold hard cash, that he'll come help me clean up the yard.

Last, a dwarf fruit tree is a great gift to give a friend or a child. Any time you plant a tree, you're not only beautifying your yard, feeding your family, and increasing your house value but you're adding oxygen to the air and removing carbon. As my arborist pals at Jonsteen Tree Nursery like to say, "We're tree advocates. We're leading the fight against nature deficit disorder!"

A PLANT RECOMMENDATION FROM THE
DIRT DIVA ROYAL HORTICULTURAL SOCIETY

Ribes sanguineum
COMMON NAME: flowering currant

This beautiful deciduous aromatic shrub can grow to 10 feet tall with gracefully arching canes that bear maple-like leaves with spikes of small pink flowers in the early spring. Its fall foliage adds red-orange autumn color. This is a fast-growing shrub and an excellent option for a lightly shaded area. For edible tart fruit to eat fresh or cooked, try *R. silvestre* (red currant) in Zones 6–9. (*R. speciosum* and *R. malvaceum* are both evergreen drought-tolerant California natives that thrive in partial shade in Zones 7–9.) The cultivar *R. rubrum* 'Red Lake' has proven to be more disease resistant than some others.

ORIGIN: western United States
HARDINESS: Zones 5–10
GROWING REQUIREMENTS: Needs little water and does its best in partial shade. Can be prone to fungal infection after many years.

THE UNIVERSAL BOTANICAL
WHAAA-WHAA RATING: 4

PART FIVE

A Seasonal Breakdown of Gardening Chores and Maintenance

Some of you are having a lifelong love affair with your garden and are happy to be coaching it along sustainably throughout the seasons. You are my star students. If only everyone could be like you. Other readers, especially my closest friends and family, just want to know *when* to do *what* in the yard and wish I would stop defending microscopic soil organisms and kitchen food scraps. "Enough with the decay cycle! Plants grow and die, and then invisible underground elves regurgitate plant nutrients. We get it," they moan and roll their eyes at me. "Now . . . *why* did my petunias die?"

Sigh. The following breakdown of seasonal gardening chores will help to remind you when to prune, tidy up, divide, plant seeds and cover crops, or add a layer of compost and mulch to your yard. It takes a few seasons, even a few years, of adding organic matter to your soil to create the healthiest, most nutrient-filled soil so that you're doing less work in your yard in the future. Like any long-term commitment, it takes work, and the more you give (in this case, garbage, organic material), the more you get back. Soon enough you'll be having conversations with your roses and hosting a pair of squirrels, Spike and Mike. Carry on, comrades!

Autumn

IF YOU BUILD IT, THEY WILL COME

What you do in the fall will help make your spring and summer flower dreams come true, so get those kids off to their first day of school and get to work in your yard. Fall is a critical time to clean up the garden. This way, you'll have fewer pests spending the winter huddling under piles of debris and less chance of disease spreading from old plants. Pick up fallen branches, pots, and rubble you've been eying all summer, saying to yourself, "I'll pick that up when I'm good and ready or, maybe in the fall." Fall is here. Pick it up so snails, slugs, insects, and fungal spores find a new skate park to hang out at and use swear words. Here are some other fall chores that your garden will thank you for later:

- Pull up dying annuals, weeds, and vegetables. Rake up leaves and add all of this to your compost pile.
- Walk around your yard and look for diseased plants: white powdery mildew, orange rust, or black spot. Pull out diseased plants or if you must keep them, prune them back hard, aiming to give them better air circulation and more sunlight. Toss all parts into

the garbage, not your compost pile, which may not be hot enough to handle those wicked spores. Rake the area around infected plants and toss infected debris into the rubbish as well.

■ Rake lawns and toss the leaves into your compost pile or into your flowerbeds. Or mow them up and scatter them on your lawn. Excellent nitrogen source! Please, please, please, stop putting them in plastic bags and sending them to our overcrowded landfills. Whoever came up with that idea is so fired!

■ Once your yard is raked and cleaned up, add a 2- or 3-inch layer of compost to your flowerbeds, and then add a 2-inch layer of mulch on top of that. This way, the millions of soil organisms underground will keep amending your soil all winter while you don't do a thing but sit indoors at your window sipping hot chocolate, dreaming about how next summer's tomato plants will surpass your evil twin sister's homegrown tomatoes. (She's not even a bona fide gardener!) Not that you're bitter . . .

■ Plant cover crops to naturally add nutrients to your soil and make your winter garden look healthy and busy. Especially plant these where you'll be growing your spring and summer vegetable garden.

■ In colder climates, dig up tender summer bulbs and store them in a bag of wood shavings or peat moss in the garage for the winter.

■ Add new grass seed to bare patches of lawn. Or, get rid of that whiny lawn and plant ground covers now or plant an eco-lawn from Wildflower Farm (www.wildflowerfarm.com). See Chapter 21 to learn how to sheet mulch for an economical and ecological way to remove your lawn.

■ In warmer climates, you can divide many spring- and summer-blooming perennials now. In colder climates (Zones 3–6) wait till early spring.

■ Plant spring-flowering bulbs and garlic.

- If you live above Zone 6 or 7, you probably have a cool-season grass and you can fertilize your lawn in the fall and the spring with an organic fertilizer high in nitrogen. (Warm-season grasses growing in warmer climates will need to be fertilized only in the spring and a few weeks later.) You can also fertilize with sifted compost spread evenly over the lawn just before rain is expected. Mow the grass a week after you fertilize, if the weather is dry. Rake the nitrogen-rich clippings around your lawn and walk away.

- Rose growers in Zones 4 and 5 should protect their roses by tying pruned canes together and building a 1-foot-tall cone of soil around each rosebush and holding it together with a mesh hardware cloth. Because I have grown to be a climate wimp from living in sunny California, I haven't done this, but my Vermont rosarian pals swear by it. Check with your local nursery if you live in an area that dips below 15°F for extended periods of time.

- Rinse garden tools in a solution of 1 part bleach to 3 parts water. Then coat them lightly with oil so they don't rust. You can also wipe them in a bucket of oiled sand that you keep in your shed, and then keep them in the shed. Don't leave them outdoors next to your putrefying garden gloves. In fact, wash and dry those gloves and put them in the shed as well.

Winter

Winter is the best time to go out in your backyard at sunrise, in your pajamas and wool sweater, simply to putter around. This is what we gardeners live for! Wander around your property checking for fallen branches from stormy weather. Remove them. Continue raking leaves and adding them to your compost pile or spreading them onto nearby flowerbeds.

- Browse gardening books and decide what you want to do differently come spring. Consider plants that are thriving throughout the winter and get more of those. Consider digging out any plants that are too needy and taking too long to bloom. You need them like a hole in the head. Tell them that. (But don't make them cry.)
- Gardeners in warmer climates (Zones 7–10) can begin pruning roses in January. Check with you local Master Gardener's desk to see when to prune in your area, if you're uncertain.
- If frost is expected, cover up your vulnerable plants at night with an old Snoopy or SF Giants or Barbie sheet placed atop

the plant with a few sticks or stakes clasped together with clothes-pins. If you don't have those exact old bedsheets, feel free to purchase Harvest Guard, which is a lightweight fabric you can find at most nurseries.

- Another option for frost is to spray your most prized plants with Cloud Cover. This product is like ChapStick for plants. Safe for edibles as well. Spray before expected frost.

- Prune most fruit trees beginning in February and if necessary, spray with organic products to deter overwintering pests and fungal spores. (Check with your local nursery about less toxic products and the best timing.)

- Drool over seed catalogs on a rainy day. Nap. Have flowery dreams. Order seeds. Nap.

- In warmer climates (Zones 7–10), sow seeds of cool-weather annuals outdoors in February such as sweet alyssum, forget-me-nots, sweet peas, bachelor buttons, calendula, columbines, lark-spur, poppies, and snapdragons. This time of year you can also take cuttings from woody perennials.

- Sow seeds indoors in cooler climates in February. Some fool-proof ones are aster, black-eyed Susan, speedwell, Shasta daisy, gaura, blanketflower, and sea thrift.

- Cut late-flowering clematis back to a foot off the ground in late winter. There are 3 different groups of clematis and 200 species, so keep the tag to know which one you have. You'll need to re-search the right time to prune.

Spring

TAKE ALL THE CREDIT.
YOUR GARDEN ROCKS!

Spring will be your busiest time in the yard. As soon as the weather begins warming up, you're back on the job. The good news is that the microorganisms underground enjoy the warmer temperatures too, so they start working with you. If you put your ear to the ground you'll hear "Whistle While You Work." Try it.

This is when you'll be pruning and dividing many perennials, but most important, take the time to get weeds under control. If you wait until weeds go to seed in the late spring, you'll be doomed. Get a hold of them in early spring and you'll be saving yourself misery for years to come.

- Pull mulch a few inches away from the main stem of roses. Let them get some air. They survived the winter!
- Consider adding another layer of compost and mulch to your vegetable garden and flowerbeds once the frosty weather has passed. (If you've grown cover crops in these areas, you may not need to add more compost. Chop up the cover crops and blend them into your soil to breakdown for a few weeks before planting

vegetables.) If you can't add a layer of compost to an entire area, you can also simply side-dress certain plants with a shovelful of compost.

- Prune roses in Zones 1–6. Warmer zones should have already pruned in January or February. If you haven't, stop tweeting that you're at Starbucks and get on with it! All zones can begin fertilizing roses organically once a month throughout the spring and summer.

- Divide crowded plantings of summer- and fall-blooming perennials such as dahlias, daylilies, Shasta daisies, hostas, and summer phlox.

- Weed like your life depended on it! Put your iPod on and hand pull weeds every 2 weeks or so. Be vigilant. Get rid of those troublemakers before they set their thousands of seeds each on your property. Go ice those hoods! Tell them the sheriff is back in town.

- Prune any summer-flowering shrubs that bloom on new growth: crape myrtle, butterfly bush (can be cut back to 1-foot stalks), many lavenders, sages, and hydrangeas (deadhead mopheads and lacecaps).

- Pinch back azaleas, camellias, and rhododendrons after they bloom, and feed with an all-purpose organic fertilizer made especially for acid-loving plants.

- Check up on your drip system. Open the lines, and let the water roll through. Check each emitter to see if there is water coming out of it or if it's clogged. Get ready to do some repair work. Breathe. Be patient. Mumbling obscenities under your breath is okay if there are no children in the vicinity. If there are, pay them a quarter a word.

- Plant summer-blooming bulbs such as dahlias, begonias, gladiolas, and tuberoses.

- Divide perennials (especially in Zones 3–5) in early spring. This is when many plants are still partially dormant, so they'll be less shocked when they get whopped in the head with the edge of your shovel.
- Plant your vegetable garden!
- Aerate the lawn. Next, fertilize your lawn with an organic fertilizer. You could simply use screened compost or buy an environmentally safe product. (I use TerraCycle's Worm Poop Lawn fertilizer. You attach the bottle to your hose. What could be more fun than worm poop from a hose? Go get some at www.shoponlygreen.com. Fire it up!) Plan to fertilize when rain is expected. A week later, when the grass has dried, mow the lawn, leaving the nitrogen-rich grass clippings on it. Rake them around and pat yourself on the back for working alongside Mother Nature.
- Check on pop-up sprinkler heads for your lawn. Make sure they're not watering the sidewalk, or my blood pressure will spike up.
- Make bouquets of roses for your friends and family. Show off, baby! You earned it. When they go on and on about what outstanding scented roses you grow, take in all the gushing and savor it. Take all the credit! Then go out to your rosebushes and quietly thank them, and promise to give them some credit next year. "Ha! Like that's going to happen," they're thinking. "What a hack!"

Summer

SCHOOL'S OUT,
SIT IN LAWN CHAIR,
SIP LEMONADE

f you've been adding compost and mulch regularly to your yard, the summer should be pretty relaxing for you. Your biggest concern will probably be making sure the plants are receiving a deep enough watering during the heat spells. If you get summer rain in your climate zone, you are so lucky!

For gardeners in drier climates, check on your drip lines every so often to see that there are no leaks or clogged emitters. If a certain plant is wilting or being attacked by pests, check that water is actually getting to it. If it's at the end of your drip line, the water pressure may be too low and the poor plant isn't getting enough water. (Boy, will you feel guilty.) Turn up the water pressure incrementally to a point where every plant is treated equal.

- Deadheading is all the rage in the summer. Keep the deadheading coming and you could possibly see a later bloom on many flowering perennials and annuals. Deadhead your lilac after it blooms to the next set of leaves, usually in late summer, to motivate next year's blossoms.

- Keep up with the weeding. Put your iPod on and hand pull weeds every 3 weeks or so. Be vigilant.
- Spray off aphids with a hose. A light spray a few days in a row will get rid of them for good.
- If your roses or lilacs become infected with powdery mildew, mix 1 tablespoon baking soda, 1 tablespoon vegetable oil, and ½ teaspoon dish soap (to make it adhere to the leaves) in 1 gallon of water and spray in the morning, every 4 to 5 days for 2 to 3 weeks, when weather is damp. Prune the center of the rose to let in more air and sunlight. This solution will stop it from spreading to other plants. It won't cure the problem completely.
- Lightly prune spring-flowering shrubs when they're done blooming.
- Plant warm-season vegetables (tomatoes, cucumbers, melons, and peppers).
- Tie or stake tall plants that need support.
- Trim evergreen hedges in June or July.
- Are your plants looking wiped out from the heat? Make sure you have a 2- to 3-inch layer of mulch around them to help hold in moisture through the hot summer weather. A foliar spray of compost tea will be appreciated now.
- Fertilize plants in pots once a month with a liquid seaweed emulsion or fish emulsion or compost tea. Water potted plants more frequently than plants in the ground, especially plants in clay pots.
- Drag your lawn chair to your favorite backyard spot, make some iced tea, and read a book or just stop and enjoy your garden. Breathe in and no matter what, see the glass half full. Think about what you are grateful for.

SOME PERENNIALS THAT WILL BE BLOOMING IN THE SUMMER

Baby's breath	Daylily	Peony
Balloon flower	Echinacea	Pincushion flower
Bee balm	Foxglove	*Rudbeckia*
Bellflower	Globe thistle	Shasta daisy
Butterfly weed	Hollyhock	Spiderwort
Campion	Larkspur	Yarrow
Coralbells	Meadowsweet	

Your Final Pep Talk

YOU DID IT!
YOU AND YOUR GARDEN
GROW UP, FINALLY

Imagine a world where everyone had a bedazzling yard overflowing with gracefully arching vines heavy from nectar-filled flowers. A native habitat flourishing with bees, butterflies, and hummingbirds. A steaming hot compost pile filled with kitchen scraps and teeming with earthworms and all their microbial cohorts. A crop of organic mixed greens emerging beneath a canopy of fruit-laden trees, and . . . where everyone listened to me. Wouldn't life be swell? Then I could lounge around in my backyard, drinking my organic, fair-trade Ethiopian decaf coffee in peace. Instead I lose sleep wondering: Am I doing enough to inspire others to become noble caretakers of our planet? How do I convince more people about the necessity of using time-honored and sustainable growing practices to regenerate our soils for future generations instead of poisoning our land for good?

Having been raised in a Manhattan high-rise apartment, I actually saw real vegetable crops and fruit orchards for the first time when I was in third grade. PS6 did its annual field trip to the Metropolitan Museum, where there was a photography exhibit about the American farmlands of Oklahoma, Nebraska, and South Dakota. All these glorious places I'd heard of but that orbited insignificantly like distant planets around the hugest of all stars, Manhattan. I knew people lived in those places (I *was* educated in New York), but I didn't know they actually grew the food that ended up on my plate. The stunning colors and aliveness in the photos made an indelible imprint on my young, impressionable mind. A bountiful fall harvest set against a background of black fertile soil, verdant fields, and cheerfully blue skies made me connect, possibly for the first time, as to the true origins of our food before it arrives at our busy metropolitan supermarket. To a die-hard city kid, this was a mind-boggling, humbling, and definitely life-transforming experience.

As little as 60 years ago there were over 6 million farms across this great country. Sadly, the number of farms now stands near 2 million. Shipping, processing, packaging, advertising, retailing of food, and the short-minded goals and seemingly irrevocable metastasis of agribusiness and corporate greed have left the American family farmer on the brink of extinction. If you ask most kids today where their food originates from, you'd probably get the name of some fast-food chain or the mega-supermarket or possibly SpongeBob's Krusty Krab Shack. The connection of food coming from the land is a way of life that is sadly and rapidly disappearing and, with it, something very deep inside of us. Mahatma Gandhi said, "To forget how to dig the earth and tend the soil is to forget ourselves."

Prince Charles, a fellow organic gardener, and I, Queen Bee of the Dirt Diva Royal Horticultural Society, share a common bond. We hear Mother Earth's voice in our heads. She speaks to us in a (fake) British accent. She says if we continue to waste our natural resources and pollute our environment, we'll fail to maintain an ecological balance. And that's when bad things happen: drought, erosion, floods, climate change . . . *Apparently, she's not big on forgiveness.* His Royal Highness, in his book *The Elements of Organic Gardening*, writes, "Our descendants are highly unlikely to thank us if it's ultimately found that we have indeed been guilty of treating nature merely as a laboratory and not as a vast, integrated, living organism." We hold our children's future in our hands.

Ecological enlightenment starts in our communities, our schools, our neighborhoods, and ultimately in our own yards. When children grow up in neighborhoods landscaped with a diversity of native plants, ornamental flowering shrubs, and edible fruits and vegetables, they learn a respect and admiration for the generous wonders and magnificent gifts of the natural world. They see their closest role models, their parents, neighbors, and teachers making wise use of local natural resources instead of wasting and contaminating them. We know how to do this. As a nation we have done it before. We just need a little nudge to get up off the couch and away from the computer. In the years between 1941 and 1943, the U.S. Department of Agriculture estimated more than 20 million Victory Gardens were planted on public and private land in the United States and 40 percent of our total produce came from those gardens. Our grandparents did it then. We can do it now.

I am proof you can learn how to garden at any age, young or old. I was 36 when I held my first earthworm (without screaming). I was consumed for many years by the cuckoo Hollywood movie industry before I even dreamed about growing my own garden. After countless failed horticultural misadventures that didn't remotely match the pictures in the plant magazine, I came to realize that home gardening is really a long series of promising earth-science experiments. Fortunately, this isn't school and you're not being graded. So loosen up a bit, have some fun, and don't be afraid to fail. (Nobody's calling your parents!) Don't be intimidated by the botanical experts at your local nursery spewing out the unpronounceable Latin names of all your favorite plants. This naming system, devised by Carl Linnaeus in the eighteenth century, rarely hints at how to say or spell a plant's scientific name. I'm certain ol' Carl is laughing in his grave.

Gardening is intuitive, therapeutic, and spiritual. Listen to what you hear when you're out in your garden. There's a voice carried on the wind that's as old as the first humans planting their first food crops. You'll enjoy great successes but will endure even more failures and sometimes it just won't make sense. The plants you coddled will die and the ones you ignored will thrive. Go with it, and remember, when in doubt, the answer usually is "compost and mulch." If you're truly lost, peek at the latest issue of *Sunset*, *Fine Gardening*, or *Organic Gardening* magazine and copy their ideas. That's what they're there for. I also give you permission to use any brilliant tip you might glean from this book and call it your own. That's how it's done in Hollywood, baby!

Remember to slow down and dawdle in your yard. The idea is to enjoy it. Sit on a garden bench and inhale. Do you smell the jasmine, honeysuckle, and scented geranium? Feel gratitude. Notice how Nature works on her own time. The plants grow silently, slowly. They follow a master design, a profound plan dating back countless centuries. When you plant a garden, you take part in a great human tradition and something inside awakens in you. I started out with an overgrown weed patch and have been continuously transforming it ever since. I often wonder why it took so long for the garden to mature, but it probably wonders the same about me. It is a work still in progress and some days it looks better than others. Yet, it's this precious connection that I've made with my garden that is such an unexpected gift. I don't give up on it, and it doesn't give up on me. It keeps me eternally optimistic and humbled by its awesome magic.

I wish you a garden that gets better year after year, and I hope that someday if we meet you'll tell me what crazy-person outfit you wear at first light each morning when you hand water your backyard potted plants. Mine is blue flannel pajama bottoms, an orange wool sweater, bright red polka-dotted rubber boots, and a brown striped Sherpa's cap.

And, lipstick.

THE DIVA'S LITTLE BLACK (GREEN) BOOK

RESOURCES FOR SHOPPING, LEARNING, COMMUNITY, AND INSPIRATION

ORGANIC GARDENING PRODUCTS AND SUPPLIES

Green Culture www.composters.com: Composters and rain barrels and other products for an enlightened planet.

Extremely Green Gardening Company www.extremelygreen.com: Specializes in organic fertilizers, pest and weed control. Arlington, MA.

Gardener's Supply Company www.gardeners.com: Gardening tools, gifts, natural pest control with fine customer service. Burlington, VT.

Happy D Ranch www.happydranch.com: Down-to-earth ideas and worm bins!

Peaceful Valley Farm and Garden Supply www.groworganic.com: Full range of organic growing supplies. Grass Valley, CA.

Planet Natural www.planetnatural.com: Earth-friendly garden supplies. Bozeman, MT.

Worm Woman www.wormwoman.com: Mary Appelhof literally wrote the book on worm composting! Advice and worm supplies.

ORGANIZATIONS PROMOTING ENVIRONMENTALLY SOUND GARDEN PRACTICES
AND PUBLIC HEALTH RESEARCH

Beyond Pesticides www.beyondpesticides.org

Pesticide Action Network North America www.panna.org

Environment and Human Health www.ehhi.org

National Pesticide Information Center http://npic.orst.edu/gen.htm

ExToxNet http://extoxnet.orst.edu.

Green Schools Initiative www.greenschools.net/index.html: Pesticide-free schools.

Environmental Working Group www.ewg.org

Union of Concerned Scientists www.ucsusa.org

World Watch Institute www.worldwatch.org

Farm Aid www.farmaid.org

A FEW GARDENING AND GREEN WEBSITES I LIKE TO VISIT

EcoMom www.ecomom.com

Garden Girl www.gardengirltv.com

Garden Rant www.gardenrant.com

National Gardening Association www.garden.org

Green Options www.greenoptions.com

Green Talk Radio www.greentalkradio.com

Learn 2 Grow www.learn2grow.com

Marin Organic www.marinorganic.com

Organic Gardening www.organicgardening.com

You Bet Your Garden www.youbetyourgarden.org

Veggie MD (Cornell University) http://vegetablemdonline.ppath.cornell.edu

SOIL TESTING

Laboratories by Mail

A & L Eastern Agricultural Lab
7621 White Pine Road
Richmond, VA 23237
804-743-9401
www.al-labs-eastern.com

Wallace Laboratories
365 Coral Circle
El Segundo, CA 90254
310-615-0116
www.bettersoils.com

Home Soil-Test Kits

Gardener's Supply Company
800-833-1412
www.gardeners.com

Mellingers
800-321-7444
www.mellingers.com

Gempler's
800-382-8473
www.gemplers.com

MASTER GARDENERS

Imagine a group of 90,000 garden geeks spread around the United States passionately dispensing scientifically based horticultural information. Holy rutabaga! Talk about an opinionated bunch! Find a local group to help advise you in your community at the American Horticultural Society's website (www.ahs.org) or www.extension.org/pages/extension_master_ gardener.

PLANT HARDINESS ZONE MAP

The U.S. Department of Agriculture produces a map of the United States that delineates 11 hardiness zones. What determines a zone is the lowest wintertime temperature. For example, in Zone 2 temperatures can fall to −50°F and lower. However, in Zone 10, the temperatures rarely ever go below 30°F. You'll see the designation in gardening books, catalogs, and magazines that reads, "Hardy to Zone 5," for example. This means the chosen plant can survive in Zone 5 and up. In Zone 4, it may freeze and wave a teary good-bye. Of course there are many microclimates incorporated into each of these zones with varied elevation and precipitation, especially in the western states, so check with your County Extension office for more local-related growing conditions. For a quick reference, you can go to the National Gardening Association website (www.garden.org/zipzone). Here you can type in your ZIP code to find your climate zone.

The following map from the Arbor Day Foundation is similar to the USDA Plant Hardiness Zone Map, but I find it easier to read.

One last thing to make your mind spin: Many nurseries in the western states use *Sunset Magazine*'s more precise Climate Zone chart, which covers 13 western states, to label their plants. This information can be found at www.sunset.com/garden/climate-zones.

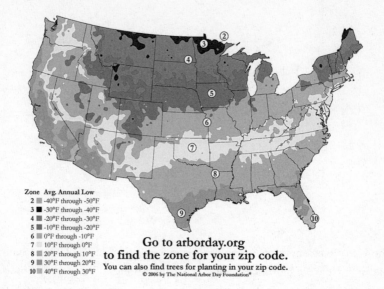

Zone Avg. Annual Low
  2 ■ -40°F through -50°F
  3 ■ -30°F through -40°F
  4 ■ -20°F through -30°F
  5 ■ -10°F through -20°F
  6 ■ 0°F through -10°F
  7 ■ 10°F through 0°F
  8 ■ 20°F through 10°F
  9 ■ 30°F through 20°F
 10 ■ 40°F through 30°F

**Go to arborday.org
to find the zone for your zip code.**
You can also find trees for planting in your zip code.
© 2006 by The National Arbor Day Foundation®

BIBLIOGRAPHY

I enjoyed almost every day, sitting in my little writing studio, nestled under a pair of giant Redwood trees, sipping Earl Grey tea, and paging through extraordinary gardening and horticultural books. My plan was to compress, simplify, and put a little clown hat on all the scientific research, jargon, and botanical gobbledygook. On those few bad days in between, I felt as if my brain were emitting smoke and were about to blow. But mostly these fine books made me want to dash outside, give the rusty ol' compost tumbler a few wild and rowdy spins, and go play in the dirt.

Brenzel, Kathleen Norris, ed. *Sunset Western Garden Book*. Menlo Park, CA: Sunset Publishing, 2007.

Bush-Brown, Louise and James. *America's Garden Book*. Edited by Howard S. Irwin, Pamela Hoenig, and Brooklyn Botanic Garden. New York: Macmillan, 1996.

Chesman, Andrea, and Louise Lloyd, eds. *The Big Book of Gardening Skills*. Pownal, VT: Storey Communications, 1993.

Ellis, Barbara W., Fern Marshall, and Ellen Phillips, eds. *Rodale's Ultimate Encyclopedia of Organic Gardening*. Emmaus, PA: Rodale, 2009.

HRH Prince Charles of Wales and Stephanie Donaldson. *The Elements of Organic Gardening*. Carlsbad, CA: Kales Press, 2007.

Pearce, Pam. *Golden Gate Gardening*. Seattle, WA: Sasquatch, 1998.
Pittenger, Dennis R., ed. *California Master Gardener Handbook*. Davis, CA: University of California Agricultural and Natural Resources, 2004.
Tidd, Debi Eglit. *Creating Healthy Gardens Naturally*. San Rafael, CA: Marin County Stormwater Pollution Prevention Program, 2007.

INDEX